DATE DUE

DEMCO 38-296

THE
VODKA
Companion
A CONNOISSEUR'S GUIDE

THE VODKA

Companion

A CONNOISSEUR'S GUIDE

DESMOND BEGG

RUNNING PRESS
PHILADELPHIA · LONDON

A QUINTET BOOK

© 1998 by Quintet Publishing Limited

998 by Running Press

d International

ters Ltd

9 8 7 6 5 4 3 2 1

Digit on the right indicates the number of this printing

ISBN 0-7624-0252-0

Library of Congress
Cataloging-in-Publication Number 97-68283

This book was designed and produced by
Quintet Publishing Limited
6 Blundell Street
London N7 9BH

Creative Director: Richard Dewing
Art Director: Silke Braun
Designer: Ian Hunt
Senior Editor: Sally Green
Editor: Andrew Armitage
Photographer: Paul Forrester

Typeset in Great Britain by
Central Southern Typesetters, Eastbourne
Manufactured in Singapore by Eray Scan Pte Ltd

This book may be ordered by mail from the publisher.
Please include $2.50 for postage and handling.
But try your bookstore first!

Running Press Book Publishers
125 South Twenty-second Street
Philadelphia, Pennsylvania 19103-4399

All gallon measurements refer to U.S. gallons

To Diana Isabel, a great mother and a great friend

Contents

PART ONE
THE STORY OF VODKA   7

Vodka Today   8

Raw Materials   11

The Arrival of Distillation in Europe   14

Distillation and Rectification   16

Filtration and Purification   21

Vodka Styles   23

Russia   25

Poland   32

Finland   37

Sweden   40

Western Europe   44

The U.S.A.   46

Flavored Vodkas   49

How to Serve and Drink Vodka   53

PART TWO
THE VODKA DIRECTORY   57

The West   58

Poland   128

Russia   156

VODKA COCKTAILS   172

VODKA WITH FOOD   185

TALL STORIES—VODKA ANECDOTES   189

Glossary   189

Index   191

Introduction

When I was first approached by a publisher to write a book on vodkas I had strong misgivings. I had tasted enough of them to know that the belief held by most people in the West that "vodka is vodka" was a myth. But what was the point of writing a book with a lot of tasting notes on a spirit that most people use as a mixer?

Now, having tasted more than a hundred different brands under reasonably clinical conditions, I am very pleased that I have. Vodka is the most widely consumed spirit in the world and there are thousands of brands, over a thousand in Poland alone. I have by no means tasted them all but what has struck me most about those that I have tasted is the enormous difference in quality and character among them. Some have been absolutely glorious. Many have been very good. Others not so good. The first intention of this book, therefore, is to persuade the reader to be far more discriminating about vodka. The second intention is even more positive. There are many vodkas that deserve far better respect than to be considered as just an alcoholic base for cocktails. There are even some that are not suitable for mixing. In Eastern Europe and the Nordic countries vodka is treated with respect and is drunk straight and chilled so that it can be fully appreciated, and some Western brands deserve the same treatment. Vodka is an unaged spirit that does not have the complexity or depth of flavor of brown spirits such as malt whisky, Cognac, or Bourbon. But it can be a very fine spirit indeed and should be appreciated as such.

Judging the merits of any spirit and writing tasting notes is a very subjective and difficult thing to do. So I do not expect the reader to agree with all my ratings or my descriptions of the different brands. It is up to the individual to make up his or her own mind, and I very much hope that you will do so. It will mean that you are beginning to differentiate between the brands and to appreciate that all vodkas are not the same.

Desmond Begg
LYMINGTON, ENGLAND

PART ONE

THE
STORY OF VODKA

Vodka Today

Vodka is the most popular spirit in the world today. Quite how much is produced and consumed across the globe is impossible to even estimate, as there are so many small, obscure brands produced and consumed locally. The panel shown opposite, however, begins to illustrate quite how popular it is. The top 15 brands sell about 171 million cases of the spirit a year, and this is only part of the picture. If you consider that Poland alone produces over a thousand different brands, then you can begin to appreciate the magnitude of vodka's undoubted popularity.

Most of the world's vodka is consumed in Eastern Europe and the Nordic countries, where it has been the traditional spirit for centuries, and in North America and Western Europe, where its large-scale consumption is a relatively new phenomenon. But how it is perceived in these two areas is very different.

Vodka drinking in the West was first made popular in the United States and the credit for this should be given to Smirnoff. The story of the Smirnoff family and how their secret formula for vodka production was eventually put into practice by a small American liquor company called Heublein is told in another chapter. But it was John G. Martin, Heublein's owner, who established an image for the spirit that it still holds today.

Vodka is the most popular spirit in the world today, widely regarded as a drink in its own right, not just for use as a mixer.

THE WORLD'S BIGGEST VODKA BRANDS

BRAND	ESTIMATED SALES (BY CASE—EACH CASE CONTAINING 2.4 US GALLONS)
Stolichnaya	60.0m.
Moskovskaya	35.0m.
Ruskaya	20.0m.
Wyborowa	18.1m.
Smirnoff	15.2m.
Absolut	5.8m.
Popov	3.2m.
Koskenkorva	2.0m.
Gordon's	2.0m.
Finlandia	1.7m.
McCormick	1.7m.
Magic Crystal	1.5m.
Kamchatka	1.2m.
Barton	1.2m.
Gorbatschow	1.2m.
Wolfschmidt	1.1m.

Martin's stroke of genius was to market vodka in the United States as a pure, very neutral spirit that could be mixed with anything. The emphasis was on mixability and versatility, on cleanliness, purity, and also elegance. This was in sharp contrast to the more macho, hairy-chested image of Scotch, Bourbon, and gin. It did not matter that the vodka first produced by the Smirnoffs in Moscow was a very different spirit—one with what the Eastern Europeans justly call "character"—which was drunk neat, well chilled, and probably with food. Martin's idea of an elegant, neutral spirit that would give orange juice or ginger beer a kick or could be mixed with vermouth took off with a bang.

This image was reinforced by Martin's genius in advertising. In the 1950s he launched a series of advertisements that was to underline the spirit's versatile, jet-set image. The most famous was one depicting a dry vodka Martini cocktail in front of the great pyramid of Egypt. Later he was to run a series linking the brand with celebrities such as the actor Walter Slezak. It is a style that the brand has remained faithful to. Today Smirnoff is depicted next to the giants of Easter Island or the Statue of Liberty, and the message is straightforward: Smirnoff vodka is an international, fashionable drink.

Other Western brands have built on these foundations. Today's wonder brand is Absolut, and its popularity has been built as much on the daring of its advertising and the elegance of its packaging as on the quality of the spirit itself. It is the same with Finlandia, the "Vodka from the top of the world," and other leading international

The famous 1950s Smirnoff jet-set image style advertisement.

brands. No matter that much of the vodka consumed in the West is of poor quality and is sold on the basis of price alone. Vodka as a spirit is imbued in the West with an image of elegance and fashion.

It all sounds very superficial, and it is. But there are signs that things are changing. Perhaps because so many flavored vodkas are hitting the market, an increasing number of people in the West are beginning to pay more attention to what they are drinking than to what kind of bottle it is presented in. And they are beginning to notice differences between the various styles of vodkas. In any good cocktail bar in New York, London, or Berlin there is now a wider range of vodkas available than ever before, and they are not just Western brands. The demand for Russian and Polish vodkas is growing as people begin to realize that not all vodkas are the same and that vodka can be served not only as a base for cocktails but as a superior spirit that should be enjoyed neat and slightly chilled so that its character and quality can be fully appreciated. There are even some bars that are making vodka a specialty, a development that would have been unheard of in John Martin's day, when the basis of vodka's popularity was that it tasted and smelled of nothing. It is a development that is to be very much encouraged.

In Eastern Europe the image of vodka is very different. In contrast to the West, where the consumption of good vodka is on the increase, in Eastern Europe, and even in Sweden and Finland, vodka consumption is on the decline. In Poland and Russia vodka is now being increasingly perceived as an old-fashioned, traditional spirit, one associated with the old political regimes and times of economic hardship when it was the only accessibly priced luxury on the market. In Eastern Europe, vodka is suffering from the same image crisis as Scotch and Bourbon are in the West. It is very much what one's parents drank, not fashionable at all.

Enormous quantities of vodka are still being consumed in Eastern Europe. But those that can afford them are looking more and more for new, Western brands that are cleaner, lighter, and purer than those produced in their own countries. Meanwhile, sales of other spirits such as Scotch, Bourbon, and Cognac are also rising. A friend of mine was recently in Warsaw and asked for a Wyborowa, only to be asked why he wanted to drink such an old-fashioned drink when he could have a good Western brand such as Smirnoff.

It is a curious reversal of roles. But it is a very positive one, one that proves that there is room for all styles of good vodka, both Eastern and Western. I can only hope that the opening up of the West to Russian and Polish tastes and flavors, and of the East to the purity, crispness, and lightness of Western vodkas, will lead to a greater awareness and appreciation of the world's most popular spirit.

Raw Materials

Vodka—clear, unflavored vodka—is a spirit made from grains or other crops such as potatoes and diluted to the required strength with water. It is then purified to a very high degree, much higher than other spirits such as Scotch or brandy. But the quality of the raw materials still has a bearing on the character of the vodka that you get in the bottle. A rye vodka may be very pure but it is still different from one made from molasses. An understanding of the raw materials used, therefore, is essential for the appreciation of vodka.

CEREALS

The traditional grain used in vodka production, especially in Eastern Europe, is rye. In Russia it was used almost exclusively until the 1870s, when other grains and potatoes began to be used more frequently, particularly in times of economic hardship. Rye, however, is still the main ingredient in the best Russian vodkas, often with small quantities of other grains such as wheat, oats, or barley thrown into the initial wash. In Poland, the world's largest rye producer, it is still in widespread use and gives the best Polish vodkas the lovely, soft, slightly sweet, and gentle aroma and flavor that is their hallmark.

Grain provides the raw material for a high percentage of vodka. The traditional grain used is rye.

Elsewhere, however, wheat has taken over as the main base grain principally because of its greater availability and lower price. High-grade wheat, which grows in abundance in North America and Western Europe, has the advantage of being comparatively easy to break down so that the starch is converted into fermentable sugars. This makes it easier to rectify to a high level of purity and neutrality, the attributes most sought after by Western distillers. Whether it is better to use whole grains with the germ and husk intact or whether these should be removed prior to the fermentation process is a vexed question among distillers. Some believe that the husks and germ add something to the spirit. Others that all that is needed is starch content to break down into sugar.

Potatoes

These are often dismissed, particularly in Russia, as an inferior base for vodka production but they have been used in parts of Eastern Europe such as the Ukraine for centuries.

Potatoes have their disadvantages. First, you need a lot of them as one ton of potatoes will produce 30 percent less vodka than a ton of grain. Secondly, they are difficult to break down and tend to produce chemicals during fermentation that are difficult to extract during rectification. Potato vodkas, therefore, do tend to be heavier and more flavorful than grain-based ones, often quite unpleasantly so. But progress has been made both in their distillation and in developing special varieties so that, when grown in the right soils and climate, they are more suitable to be converted into a spirit. The result is that some modern potato vodkas are very good but only if you like a heavier style.

Potatoes have been used to make vodka in parts of Eastern Europe for centuries.

Molasses

This is the syrup extracted from raw sugar during the refining process and is used quite frequently in the West. Spanish distillers, for example, often use molasses from sugarbeet or sugarcane to make base spirit. In the past it was used principally because it was cheap, but the glut of grain on Western markets and the ready availability of high-quality grain spirit has eroded this advantage. In my experience, while vodkas made from molasses have clean and pure aromas, they do tend to be a little bit sweeter on the palate than those made with grain.

WATER

"Water breathes life into vodka" is an old Polish saying, and there is no doubt that it is one of vodka's most important ingredients. Think of it in this way: in most bottles of vodka water accounts for some 60 percent of its contents. The days when vodka was diluted to the required strength by adding water from the local pond or river have long since disappeared. Today most vodka distillers use water from their own wells and then put it through a rigorous purification process.

To produce good vodka the water has to be softened by having all the hard materials, notably the calcium ions and other hard minerals, removed. This is achieved by putting it through deionization columns and, in many cases, then through a further purification process such as pumping it through activated carbon or layers of sand. Ideally the water should have less than 0.00015 ounces of dissolved minerals per 0.27 gallons and will be as pure as distilled water. In the past distilled water was often used, but this tended to produce vodkas that were duller and less bright. It is also a comparatively expensive method so is now seldom used.

If bad, contaminated water is added to the rectified spirit, the vodka will not be as smooth as it should be and it can detract from its clean aroma and taste. There is also the danger of discoloration, since some materials frequently found in water, such as iron, can turn in color and impart this to the vodka.

Water accounts for some 60 percent of vodka's content. Not surprisingly, it has to go through a rigorous purification process before it can be used.

The Arrival of Distillation in Europe

It is impossible to determine exactly when or how humankind first discovered distillation. Most historical evidence, however, indicates that the first distillations were carried out in the Middle East, where perfume makers in Mesopotamia used it to extract the aromatic oils from plants and flowers as early as 3500 B.C. From there the skill appears to have spread both East and West. The Chinese were using distilled rice wine in the production of gunpowder by 1000 B.C. A thousand years later distillation was known in Alexandria, Sabur, and Damascus where it was used to make products such as lamp fuel, solvent, and disinfectant.

The Greeks and the Romans discovered ways of separating the contents of liquids, but a basic form of distillation as we know it today was probably introduced to Europe by the Arabs who swept into the Iberian peninsula in the eighth century. This would explain the Arabic origin of many of the terms used in the process, such as *al cohol* (or *al kuhul*) and *al embic,* meaning a still. From there their knowledge could have spread northward into the heart of the continent.

Arab scholars continued to experiment with the production of alcohol and its properties well into the tenth century. In other parts of Europe, however, the Dark Ages fell over the continent and distillation, along with many other aspects of civilization, was all but forgotten.

It is now the turn of the Irish to come into the picture. From the sixth to the ninth centuries the monasteries of Ireland were havens of learning in an otherwise dark world and their monks kept the secrets of distillation alive. After A.D. 1000 they returned to the continent as missionaries and distillation began again in the monasteries they

In 1334 Arnold de Villeneuve produced the first recorded wine distillate in Northern Italy. Fifty years later this grape spirit, or *Aqua Vitae* reached Northeastern Europe.

founded. By A.D. 1100 it is known beyond all doubt that alcohol was being produced by distillation in Northern Italy. In 1334 Arnold de Villeneuve produced the first recorded brandy or wine distillate meant for consumption in Provence.

It was to be at least 50 years before this grape spirit or *aqua vitae*, the water of life, was to reach Northeastern Europe. Genoese traders are known to have introduced it to the Russian court toward the end of the fourteenth century, but it made little initial impact and it was to take even longer for the people of the region to start distilling for themselves.

Quite where and when this was first done is a question that has been argued over for years. Was it in Poland or was it in Russia? We will probably never know exactly. All we do know is that spirits distilled from local grains, probably wheat, made their first appearance in the region sometime in the second half of the fifteenth century or the beginning of the sixteenth. No doubt these were very poorly distilled and were comparatively light in alcohol. But they provided a basis from which what we know as vodka today was to evolve.

The first spirits distilled from grain were no doubt poorly distilled and light in alcohol, but they formed the base of the vodka we know today.

Distillation and Rectification

Put simply, distillation is the extraction of alcohol from a low strength alcoholic liquid to make it into a stronger one. The *Cognacais* and other brandy distillers do it with wine. The *Tequileros* of Mexico with *pulque*, a beverage made by fermenting the juices of the agave plant. And the vodka distillers do it with a liquid called a wash, made by fermenting a mixture of grain or other crops and water. The first stage of vodka production, therefore, is the preparation of the wash, a beerlike liquid with a comparatively low level of alcohol.

The grain or potatoes are first crushed and mixed with water. They are then heated up to convert their starch into sugar and the result is a thick, sweet liquid known as the wort. When yeast is added this ferments and produces a wash with an alcoholic strength of about 6–8 percent. Distillation then converts this into what is known as raw spirit.

The alcoholic strength of a liquid can be increased because alcohol and water boil at different temperatures, 172°F and 212°F respectively. This, it would seem, should make it very easy to extract the alcohol from a liquid: just heat it up to 172°F and allow all the alcohol to vaporize, bring it back to liquid form in a condenser and that's that. Unfortunately it is not that simple. This is because water vaporizes even at normal temperatures so, by the time it is heated to 172°F, it is giving out a lot of steam that mixes with the vaporized alcohol. The distiller, therefore, has to capture that part of the vapor that is highest in alcohol and then proceed to distill it again.

The earliest forms of distillation took place in what are known as pot stills. These are still widely used in the Scotch and Cognac industries and are nothing more than huge copper cauldrons that close at the top into a V-shaped funnel. The wash is heated inside them and, as the heat intensifies, it begins to release its vapors. This first fraction of the distillation, however, tends to contain a considerable amount of impurities that the distiller does not want, and the last fraction, produced as the heat rises toward 172°, contains a considerable amount of water vapor. The first and final fractions, therefore, tend to be discarded while the middle part is retained.

This is what the earliest distillers will have produced. An alcoholic beverage that still contains impurities and with an alcoholic strength of about 40 proof. It was not until much later that it occurred to someone to take that middle fraction and distill it again, so reducing the content of impurities still further and raising the alcoholic level yet again to reach about 120 proof.

Old distilling apparatus. The earliest forms of distillation took place in what are known as pot stills and they are still in use in the vodka industry today.

Pot stills are still used in the vodka industry today as they give a spirit smoothness. But most vodka is now distilled in what are known as continuous, patent, or Coffey stills, which are considerably more efficient. (The Coffey still is named after its Irish inventor, Aeneas Coffey.) These also work on the basis that, when the wash is heated, its different components (not only alcohol and water) boil and begin to vaporize at different temperatures. Methanol, for example, vaporizes at a relatively low temperature, while fusel oil, an important ingredient in the vodka wash, does so only at a considerably higher one. The continuous still enables the distiller to separate all of these, as well as the water and the alcohol, in a single process.

The basic continuous still consists of two columns: the analyzer and the rectifier (see page 19). These are divided into horizontal compartments. Hot steam is introduced into the bottom of the analyzer and moves upward from compartment to compartment heating them on the way. At the same time a trickle of wash is introduced, via the rectifier,

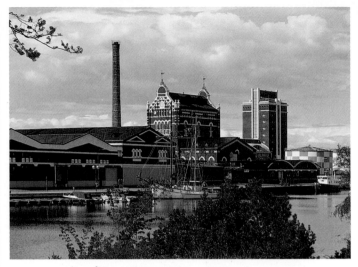

The distillery in Åhus, southern Sweden, where Absolut is made. Distillation converts wash produced by crushed and heated grain or potatoes into raw spirit.

into the top and falls onto the plates separating the compartments that have been heated by the rising steam. This heats the wash and the alcohol begins to vaporize so that, by the time the descending wash falls to the bottom of the column, most of its alcohol has been extracted and it is syphoned off. Meanwhile, the spirit vapors and remaining steam escape from the top of the column into a pipe that channels them into the bottom of the rectifier.

At this stage what you have is raw spirit containing most of the alcohol of the wash but also a considerable amount of impurities. It is the job of the rectifier to remove these impurities, leaving the distiller with the pure alcohol.

The rectifier, too, is divided into a number of compartments by perforated plates, sometimes as many as 40. It also contains the pipe taking the wash into the analyzer. When it first enters the rectifier it is cold but, as it snakes its way down the column, it begins to be warmed up by the hot, rising spirit vapors and steam from the analyzer. These, in turn, begin to be cooled by the pipe and the vapors mostly water at first begin to condense, dropping to the bottom of the column where they are easily syphoned off.

As the vapors rise further it is the alcohol fraction that begins to condense and, by inserting a plate that is not perforated (known as the spirit plate) at just the right height in the column, the distiller extracts the fraction of clean, high-strength spirit that he wants.

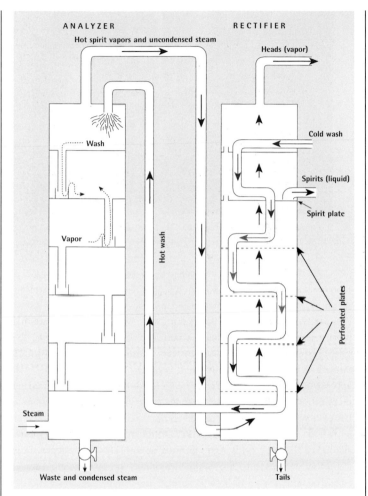

ANALYZER · RECTIFIER

Hot spirit vapors and uncondensed steam

Heads (vapor)

Wash

Cold wash

Vapor

Spirits (liquid)

Spirit plate

Hot wash

Perforated plates

Steam

Waste and condensed steam

Tails

Most vodka is distilled in the Coffey, patent or continuous still, named after its Irish inventor, Aeneas Coffey. It consists of two columns, the analyzer and the rectifier.

The basic, two-column continuous still was first used in the second half of the nineteenth century. Since then the system has been further perfected. Modern stills tend to have more than two columns, some of which do the same job again and redistill or rerectify the spirit several times, while others extract even more alcohol by recycling the heads and tails. The result is a highly efficient system, producing very pure and clean spirit of an alcoholic strength of 180 proof or over.

Much, however, can go wrong with distillation and rectification. Financial pressures being what they are today, both processes are often

The wash enters rectification columns where the alcohol fraction begins to condense and can then be extracted by the distiller by means of a "spirit plate."

just done too fast and produce vodkas with very discernible faults. For some vodka producers the problem is compounded by the fact that they do not do their own initial distillation and buy raw alcohol, which they then rectify. This gives them less control over the production process.

Hurried distillation can lead to several problems. For example, the wash can be introduced into the still when it has not been fully fermented and still contains some sugars. These burn inside the apparatus and release diacetyl, which is never completely removed by rectification and give the final vodka a smell of toffee or caramel. Unspent yeasts also burn in distillation and release what are known as Bs, which smell slightly meaty and unpleasant. While hurried rectification usually ends with the apparatus being unable to extract some impurities such as amyl alcohol, which smells of nail-enamel remover, or DMTs, which smell of boiled cabbage. Too much residual fusel oil— a thick, oily substance that makes the vodka smoother in tiny quantities—makes the vodka heavier and more greasy.

There are many vodkas on the market that have one or several of these faults. But don't take my word for it. You can judge the quality of a vodka's production by cutting one measure of vodka at room temperature with two of pure, bottled, still water such as Evian in a wineglass and then nosing it carefully after you have swirled it to release the aromas. Most faults will then become so apparent that they will scream at you.

After distillation and rectification the vodka is reduced to the required strength with the addition of water and then goes for further filtration and purification.

Filtration and Purification

More than any other spirit vodka prides itself in its purity. Where other distillers leave some congeners (flavoring elements) in their spirit to give them aroma, taste, and character, the vodka distiller does his or her utmost to remove these and produce as clean a product as possible. Most impurities are removed by proper distillation and rectification. But vodka is then subjected to further filtration with the result that, while Scotch and Cognac have about 0.10 ounces of congeners per 0.265 gallons well-purified vodka has only about 30.

Perhaps because early distillation procedures were so efficient and allowed so many impurities to remain in the spirit, vodka distillers have been experimenting with different methods of filtration from the very beginning. One of the earliest methods, for example, was to put the newly distilled spirit out into the cold. Some of the impurities, probably not very many, would then freeze and fall to the bottom so that the cleaner spirit could then be syphoned off from the top.

Slowly, however, more efficient methods were developed. Coagulants, such as egg white and milk, were added to the spirit. Or the spirit was poured through layers of materials such as felt and sand (used by the

Filtration columns. After distillation and rectification, vodka is further purified by filtrations, leaving it with a fraction of the congeners found in other spirits.

Romans), different types of cloth, even broken pottery. Today the most widely used material is charcoal, which the Russians claim they have been using since the fifteenth century.

Charcoal, or its derivative carbon, is a highly absorbent material, particularly if it is made from hardwoods such as beech or oak. In Russia the traditional wood used is the birch, from which charcoal has been made for centuries, not only for producing vodka but also for fueling samovars. These days the charcoal is "activated," or heated up to temperatures in excess of 1,000°F, when it becomes like a sponge. It is then packed into column filters in granules with the large, almost pebble-sized ones at the bottom and increasingly smaller ones on top. The vodka is pumped through the columns, preferably upward, since, if the spirit is allowed to trickle down from the top, it soon creates small channels through which it can pour relatively freely.

This can be a lengthy business. The Pierre Smirnoff Company, for example, claims that it pumps its vodka through 10 column filters and that each drop passes through seven tons of charcoal, a process that takes about eight hours. When the vodka emerges it is crystal-clear and bright. Then there is a last filtration just before bottling to remove any final floaters, usually through a membrane filter or a cartridge one packed with paper sheet filters that will remove any particle up to the size of a micron—and that's only about 0.000039 of an inch.

Charcoal filtration, however, has to be controlled. Because it is such an efficient process, the charcoal does eventually become saturated with impurities and loses its absorbent qualities. The column filter then has to be cleaned with steam, a process that some inefficient distillers do not do often enough.

All this takes time and effort and some distillers will tell you that it is overdone. If a spirit is well distilled and rectified several times, they argue, then it will be pure enough when it comes out of the still. What is undeniable is that well-made vodka is the purest potable spirit known.

It is often said, quite rightly, that vodka gives you less of a hangover than other spirits and this is because all those substances that lead to headaches and nausea are left behind. When you drink a vodka you are basically drinking pure alcohol and water. When you drink a glass of Scotch or Cognac you are also drinking minute quantities of a lot of other materials, including those that the spirit leaches out of the wood during its aging in the barrel.

So next time you have a glass of vodka too many but still wake up the next day with a clear head, think of the generations of vodka distillers whose hard work, tenacity, and experimentation have enabled them to produce a spirit of incomparable purity.

Vodka Styles

Vodka styles vary enormously; Western vodkas are valued for a totally clean taste, whereas vodkas produced in Eastern Europe have a distinct "character."

Anyone who believes that "vodka is vodka" need only go through one quick, and very interesting, exercise. Take a bottle each of a good Western brand, say a Royalty or a Tanqueray Sterling—any of those highly recommended in the Directory—and pour some into a small glass. Then take a good Polish brand—go for the classic and highly characteristic Wyborowa or one of the new designer brands like Chopin or Krowleska—and serve the same amount in a similar glass. Finally, take a good Russian brand, a Stolichnaya or a Moskovskaya, and do the same.

Line up the three glasses at room temperature, nose them carefully, and then taste. What looked like identical vodkas will suddenly reveal totally different characteristics.

THE WESTERN STYLE

Vodka producers in Western Europe, Scandinavia, and North America judge their products on their purity and cleanliness. A totally neutral nose with a taste that reveals no more than a totally clean taste of alcohol is what they prize the most. Combine this with smoothness and you have the ultimate Western vodka.

This is achieved by a very high standard of distillation and rectification. With years of profitable trading behind them, Western distillers have been able to invest large amounts in their production technology and can produce vodkas with only minute traces of congeners (taste and smell elements). U.S. vodkas in particular tend to stand out because of their neutrality of smell and taste, despite often being let down by other factors.

THE POLISH STYLE

Polish distillers also pride themselves on the purity of their product and, when compared with other spirits such as gin, whisky, or brandy, they are right. At the same time Polish vodkas are more flavorful and have far more aroma than those from the West. The best have a wonderfully gentle, slightly sweet aroma that immediately betrays their rye origins, and are soft on the palate, with a lingering sweetness that avoids being cloying. They are also slightly more oily than the Western brands, although not as much as the Russians. The Poles will never quite bring themselves to admit that this is the result of a greater quantity of remaining congeners. They call it "character" rather than flavor and still insist that their vodka is totally pure.

RUSSIAN VODKAS

It is the same with the Russians. Russian vodkas also have "character" but they tend not to be as sweet as their Polish counterparts. Good Russian vodka is very smooth with little mouth burn or needle, usually because a certain amount of fusel oil gets through the distillation and rectification. Fusel oil is a greasy, rather thick ingredient that is perfectly palatable in small quantities and gives vodka a slightly oily, smooth feel in the mouth. Russian vodka is also quite pungent and flavorful but does not have the sweetness of Polish vodkas.

When you taste the three styles at the same time and compare one with the others, the differences between them become obvious. On the one hand you have the neutral but light and crisp Western style. On the other the heavier and more characterful Polish and Russian styles. Which one is the best is obviously a matter of individual taste. But it makes one wonder why the distillers of Eastern Europe do not just admit that their vodkas are more characterful, if less pure, than those that are produced in the West.

Unscrew a bottle of a vodka brand you have never tried, and see if you can taste the quite striking difference between Western and Polish or Russian vodkas.

Russia

Whether vodka was first produced in Russia or in Poland is a question charged with political tension and national pride. Both countries argue their cases passionately and it is not the aim of this book to support either side. What has to be said is that more research has been done, or at least has been published, on the origins of vodka in Russia than in Poland. Fired by a determination to prove that vodka was a Russian invention, the academic William Pokhlebkin has combed through huge amounts of historical material and emerged with a convincing argument to support the Russian case.

Although it was not to be called vodka officially until the late nineteenth century, a cereal-based spirit was certainly distilled in Russia in the middle of the fifteenth century. Pokhlebkin sets the date at between 1448 and 1478 and goes so far as to suggest that it could have been in the Chudov monastery in Moscow (see p.185). A combination of developments during this period, he argues, made the distillation of the first vodka not only possible but highly probable.

First, the introduction of the highly efficient three-field system of agriculture in the first half of the fifteenth century resulted in a surplus of grain in the Moscow state. This meant that while all grain stocks in other Eastern European countries were needed to feed the populace, in Russia there was enough both to make bread and to begin distilling in significant quantities.

A grain-based spirit was distilled in Russia as early as the fifteenth century.

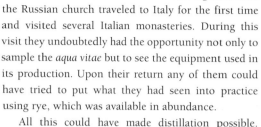

Aqua vitae, a spirit made from wine, had been known in Russia since the late fourteenth century, when it had first been shown to the court by Genoese merchants. Then toward the end of the 1430s a legation from the Russian church traveled to Italy for the first time and visited several Italian monasteries. During this visit they undoubtedly had the opportunity not only to sample the *aqua vitae* but to see the equipment used in its production. Upon their return any of them could have tried to put what they had seen into practice using rye, which was available in abundance.

All this could have made distillation possible. What makes it all the more probable is evidence of a far more chilling nature. From the accounts of contemporary observers and historians, it seems that Russia was swept by what Pokhlebkin describes as "an abrupt change ... in morals and manners which became coarsened to a striking degree." Between 1440 and 1460 new and harsher types of state repressions were introduced. Prisoners of war began to be humiliated and executed. There was a rise in civil unrest and an increase in brutal rioting among the urban poor. In Pokhlebkin's words, "There is a basis for linking these phenomena, if not completely then at least to a significant degree, with the dramatic spread of drunkenness; and above all with the change in the character of drunkenness, which now evoked not merriment but brutality. This too provides grounds for suggesting that changes had taken place in the character of alcoholic drinks."

Many will believe this theory to be fanciful and we cannot ignore the political motivation behind it. However, what is certain is that in 1474 a monopoly was imposed on the production and sale of the spirit in the state of Moscow. This indicates that its production and consumption had by then become widespread enough to merit state attention either because its influence was beginning

Early Vodka bottle. Vodka was originally called "water (*voda*) of life."

to be disruptive or because it saw it as a potentially lucrative source of state revenue. By the beginning of the sixteenth century, Moscow was producing enough to be able to export to Sweden and Estonia.

The state's direct control of vodka production and its sale was to ebb and flow for the next 250 years throughout Russia and its growing empire. From the 1530s to 1648, for example, the system of the "Czar's Taverns" was imposed. This made the tavern keepers, elected by the community and answerable to the government, responsible for all sales and production, with distilling often taking place in the taverns themselves. The system, however, was widely abused and the falling quality of vodka, growing indebtedness of the urban poor to the keepers, and widespread crop failures in rural areas due to drunkenness led to the "tavern revolts" of 1648. These were put down by the Czar Aleksey Mikhailovich who then introduced some reforms to the system but by 1681 a strict state monopoly on production was again reintroduced.

It was brought to an end at the beginning of the eighteenth century by Peter I ("the Great") who had realized that greater revenues for the state, which he very desperately needed to finance his constant wars, could be achieved

Early Smirnoff label, showing the imperial crests that meant "by appointment to the Czar."

by allowing freedom of distillation while at the same time imposing taxes on the distillers, their equipment, and their production. Large-scale vodka production followed.

The next important date in the history of Russian vodka was 1765, when Catherine II established a two-tier system of production. The privilege to distill was granted on one level to the gentry, which began to supply its own needs, those of the court, and of their own peasantry. And a system of state distilleries was set up to supply the rest of society, namely the clergy, the merchant class—who had been active in production since early in the century—and the urban poor.

The first tier ushered in a golden era for Russian vodka. Free from any economic constraints, the Russian nobility were soon producing vodka of spectacular quality. Before the arrival of distilling, Russian brewers of mead and beer had developed some sophisticated production

In 1765 Catherine II granted the privilege to distill to the gentry, those of the court, and their own peasantry. State distilleries supplied the rest of society.

techniques, particularly in the fields of filtration and purification. Filtration through river sand, felt, and even birchwood charcoal were already known. So too was purification with the help of coagulants such as milk, egg white, and isinglass, which coat impurities and either lift them to the surface of the spirit or precipitate them to the bottom, where they can be funneled off.

With no need to spare expense, the nobility used these expensive products in abundance. They could also use the best grain from their own crops—which during this period was mostly rye. And they could infuse their wonderfully pure spirit with the highest-quality materials such as cherries and other fruits, hazelnuts, juniper, mint, and aniseed. For most noble households the quality of its vodka became a matter of pride and, by the end of the eighteenth century, Russian vodka had reached the highest quality possible for a home-produced spirit. Its prestige rose to dizzying peaks, even in Western Europe, to which it had begun to be exported.

At the lower level, however, the development of vodka was not as happy. To begin with, the state distilleries produced a vodka that was of reasonable quality. But their position was soon undermined by the creation of the "chambers of beverages," institutions set up to collect the vodka and deliver it to

Moscow's oldest vodka plant. Vodka drinking is a way of life in Russia.

the state, which then put it on the market. If the supply from the state distilleries was insufficient to satisfy demand, the chambers could order from alternative sources, namely brokers who bought inferior vodka from private, usually landowning, distillers. The concessionaires made it increasingly worthwhile for the chambers to buy from them rather than the state distilleries and, starved of orders, these had virtually disappeared by the turn of the century.

Private distilling, which evolved quite separately from that of the gentry—and which the government tried periodically to control over the next century—was to have disastrous effects on the very fabric of Russian society. As it fell increasingly into avaricious and unscrupulous hands, the general standard of quality of vodka in Russia fell dramatically. In the early part of the nineteenth century cheap but low-quality vodka from Poland and schnapps from Germany began to filter into western Russia. Made on an industrial scale and using cheaper raw materials (mostly potatoes) than the traditional Russian rye, these forced the private Russian distillers to follow suit. Badly produced, impure, and harmful vodka filled the market, leading to an increase in drunkenness and alcoholism. It was not until the 1880s that the authorities, aware of the growing calamity, began to look seriously at ways of controlling the quality of vodka available to most of the people.

At first they tried to reduce the number of private distilleries in Russia and these fell from 5,000 in 1860 to about 2,000 in 1890. When this was seen to be ineffective, a full state monopoly was imposed in 1890. In the meantime efforts were already under way to improve production methods in what was left of the state distilleries, whose share of national production had fallen to 7 percent of total by 1870. Rectification was introduced to the state system in 1880. Four years later a "Technical Committee," made up of prominent scientists, was set

Drunkenness amongst the peasantry was common in Russia until 1917, when, after the Revolution, the Bolsheviks banned distillation.

up to find ways of improving quality. By the beginning of the twentieth century all state distilleries had adopted the same technology and used a standard production method.

Widespread drunkenness continued until 1917 when, believing that it degraded the working class, the Bolsheviks prohibited the distillation of vodka after the Revolution. From being commonplace, drunkenness became a shameful and contemptible act and the disapproval of alcohol soon became a prerequisite to being a good Communist. This attitude was to persist even after there was a partial lifting of the prohibition in 1924, when the sale of light alcoholic beverages such as wine and beer was permitted once again, and 1936, when small quantities of vodka began to be produced once again.

For the Russian people, however, this was to be a brief respite. In 1943, almost immediately after the victory at Stalingrad, a ration of around 3 fluid ounces of vodka began to be distributed to the Red Army. By 1945 almost the entire male population of the U.S.S.R. was in uniform, so the habit of drinking vodka swept across the country again after demobilization. During the 1950s and 1960s the price of vodka was kept deliberately low and drunkenness became widespread again, particularly among workers in heavy industries and even among the female workers in the textile industry. Although there were severe penalties against drunkenness in public places, the government did little to turn the tide.

It was not until the advent of *perestroika* in the 1980s that the government launched a determined campaign against heavy drinking. Even then, however, little was done toward educating the public in the dangers of overdrinking and the rehabilitation of alcoholics.

Vodka drinking has become so much part of life in Russian society that the campaign has had only a limited effect. It is estimated that the Russians still drink nearly 32 pints of vodka per capita per year, nearly twice the amount consumed in hard-drinking Poland. And that is not taking into account the huge quantities imported illegally. Furthermore, the age-old problem of low-quality illegal distilling has still not been wiped out, despite the best government efforts: in recent years the government has closed down some 1,700 illegal distilleries in Moscow alone, but sadly, this was not before around 50,000 Russians died as a result of drinking poisoned vodka.

VASSILISA THE BEAUTIFUL.

Vassilisa set out for the forest, trembling as she walked.

All of a sudden a man clad in red and mounted on a red horse came galloping by, and the sun began to rise.

Legends from Russia

ONLY VODKA FROM RUSSIA IS GENUINE RUSSIAN VODKA

Two well-known brands achieve legendary status in an advertisement.

It makes for depressing reading. But it must not detract from the fact that, drawing from its long traditions, Russia does produce some of the most outstanding vodkas in the world, of immense character and quality. These come from strictly controlled distilleries such as the Kristall in Moscow and the Livis in St Petersburg. All of these are shareholders in the export agency Sojuzplodoimport, which exports them to the West.

Stolichnaya is, perhaps, the best known of Russian brands. But, distilled in Moscow, the clear, unflavored Moskovskaya is, perhaps, the classic brand and, in Russia, it is used as a quality benchmark against which all other vodkas are judged. Then there are wonderfully flavored brands such as Okhotnichya, the "Hunter's vodka," and the pepper-flavored Pertsovka as well as the wonderfully romantic Sibirskaya, distilled in the frozen wastes of Siberia and filtered through silver-birch charcoal. Finally, there is the recently launched Smirnoff Black, distilled in the Kristall distillery by a thoroughly Western company. It is a range in which the Russians, quite rightly, take enormous pride. And it is thoroughly worth discovering.

Poland

If any country can contest Russia's claim to be the home of vodka, it is Poland. The problem for Poland, however, is that a Polish national champion with the patience and stature, let alone the patriotic zeal, of William Pokhlebkin has yet to emerge. Sadly, very little of any consequence has been published on the origins and development of vodka distillation in the country.

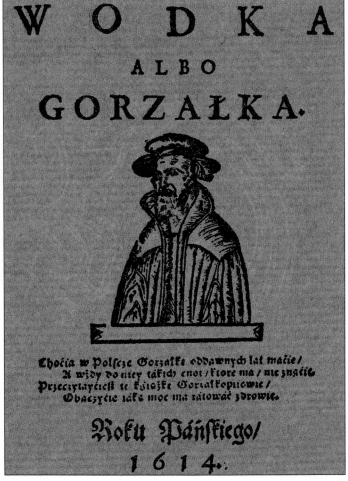

The distilling of vodka, originally known as *gorzalka*, grew in importance as a national industry from the sixteenth to the end of the eighteenth century.

There are references to vodka's being produced and consumed in Poland as early as the fourteenth century in Polish literature, namely in the works of the authors Golebiowski and Ostrowska-Szymaska, and this does reinforce the country's claim to be vodka's birthplace. But real proof of its existence does not emerge until the reign of King Jan Olbracht, who first gave the Polish people the right to distill and sell it. Then in 1564 and 1565 the first taxation on vodka distillation, the equipment used, and on its retailing was imposed, suggesting that the spirit was by then produced in significant quantities.

Originally vodka as an alcoholic beverage was known by the name of *gorzalka* and was probably made from the traditional rye or another grain. How it was drunk nobody knows. The word vodka or *wodka*, a Polish diminutive for "water," was used at the time for medicinal spirits such as tonics, refreshers, and remedies. These were usually spirits with a low alcoholic content and additives such as herbs and were consumed in small quantities, usually before breakfast, or just rubbed into aching parts of the body. Vodka was also a term used for other products. "Flavored vodkas" or fragrant waters were also produced by infusing the spirit with aromatic herbs or extracts, and were used as perfumes. In his 1534 treatise "Herbal" the scientist Falimirz refers to "vodka for washing a chin after shaving." Slowly, however, the word vodka began to supplant *gorzalka* as the term used to denote the spirit consumed for pleasure, and by the eighteenth century the two terms were used interchangeably.

In the meantime, from the sixteenth century to the end of the eighteenth, vodka distilling grew in importance and became a significant national industry. In 1572 the privilege to distill vodka was given to the aristocracy whereupon most manor houses set up their own still to distill vodka according to their own secret recipe and then sold it to the peasantry and passing travelers. The monasteries, too, were often centers of production.

Vodka distillation on a significant scale, however, was developed in the cities. It is known to have been produced in large quantities in Krakow as early as 1550, from where it was exported as far as Silesia. It was the city of Poznan, however, that became the country's most important center of production. According to early documents there were 49 distilleries in the city by 1580 and merchants from all over the country came to buy vodka.

Poznan's rise continued in the eighteenth century and its distilleries produced not only vodka but liqueurs and mead. In 1768 another distillery was built in the Grobla suburb, and trade continued to flourish. Vodka was shipped through Gdansk to St Petersburg in Russia,

Vodka drinking in Poland is rich in history, legend, and tradition. Polish literature refers to vodka being consumed as early as the fourteenth century.

by river and sea to Vienna and Wroclaw. German merchants took it to Silesia and farther afield. By the end of the century it was also exported to Moldavia, Hungary, and the coasts of the Black Sea.

Perhaps it has something to do with the climate, or with the character of the Polish people and their turbulent history, but vodka drinking became a way of life in Poland, a tradition that has survived to this day. A Frisian traveller in 1672 noted of the Poles that, "Especially they find taste in vodka, which in Polish 'gorzalka' and in their Latin 'Crematum' they call. Even the greatest aristocrats carry it with them in small cases and must have a drink almost every hour."

Another literary source, the Polish national poem "Pan Tadeusz" written by Adam Mickiewicz, describes the drinking of large cups of vodka by hunters after a big shoot, with the vodka chilled in snowdrifts and drunk after a plateful of *bigos*, a type of sauerkraut and Poland's national dish.

The logo of the Poznan distillery, the largest in Poland, built in 1823.

Poland was partitioned by Russia, Austria, and Prussia in 1772. By then vodka had spread such strong roots that its production and consumption continued to flourish throughout the one and a half centuries of occupation. The distillery that stands on the outskirts of Poznan today (the largest in Poland), for example, was built in

1823 by a Prussian cavalry regiment. Parts of the country's second largest at Zielona Góra were built in the 1880s.

Improvements to distilling equipment continued apace and new raw materials such as potatoes and sugarbeet joined the traditional rye as the basis of production.

Poland regained its independence at the end of the World War One. The Polish alcohol monopoly was set up in 1919 to oversee the production and commercialization of all alcoholic beverages and it survived until the country's defeat by the Germans in 1939. Then the post-war Communist regime introduced similar institutions to control all aspects of vodka production and its commercialization. Production was controlled by the Polmos, the Polish Spirits Monopoly, and its sale and distribution were controlled by other government bodies. Exports, for example, were handled by the Agros Foreign Trade Enterprise.

Today much of this structure has been swept away. The Polmos has been broken up into its 25 component parts which, although still government-owned, are now independent companies. Most of these "factories," as they are known in Poland, buy in raw spirit (made mostly from rye, although some are made from potatoes) from about 500 small agricultural distilleries and rectify, dilute, filter, and bottle it. They then have the right to sell it to whoever they wish, although the rights to some of the leading brands such as Wyborowa and Zubrowka on foreign markets are owned by Agros, now a company listed on the Warsaw stock exchange.

For this reason, many of the Polmoses have started to launch their own brands and some, the "prestige" ones, are

An advertisement for Polmos Krakow. There are 25 government-owned Polmoses.

high in quality and price and superbly packaged. Polmos Poznan, for example, has its superb Premium brand, Polmos Zielona Góra has Krowleska, and Polmos Krakow has Fiddler. It is estimated that there are now about a thousand different brands of Polish vodka on the market.

The "prestige" brands will undoubtedly become the vodka industry's equivalent of malt whisky and have added a welcome new dimension to the Polish industry. There is also a wide selection of interesting flavored vodkas, which includes the semisweet, cherry-flavored Wísniówka and the rowanberry-flavored Jarzębiak. It has the unique Zubrowka, flavored with bison grass. And in Wyborowa, said to be world's largest-selling vodka, it has a superb rye brand that personifies both the quality and character of high-quality Polish vodka. It is a range worthy of Poland's long traditions of vodka distilling and of its great history as a leading vodka producer.

Zubrowka is one of the Polish vodka industry's prestige brands.

Finland

It is generally believed that the secrets of vodka distillation were introduced into Finland by mercenaries returning home from European wars in the sixteenth century. With an abundance of grain from the central part of the country and plenty of pure water, vodka production blossomed and the Finns quickly took to drinking it. Within a hundred years it had supplanted beer as the country's national drink and distilling became an important part of Finnish life with most of the production coming from small, privately owned copper pot stills.

Then in 1756 there was a shortage of grain and the distillation of spirits was prohibited. Finland at that time in its history was part of the Swedish empire, and shortly afterwards the right to distill became the property of the Swedish crown, and dozens of royal distilleries were built across the country.

It was another shortage, this time of yeast, that triggered off the next important development. By the 1880s the country's only yeast factory was unable to keep up with demand created by the burgeoning vodka industry, and plans were made to build another. The site chosen was the Rajamäki manor, some 28 miles from Helsinki, and the production of baker's yeast began in 1888. Because of the purity of the water from its spring, however, it also began to produce spirits soon afterwards and, by the turn of the century, Rajamäki had become the largest of Finland's 27 distilleries. It was also the best-equipped with what was at the time state-of-the-art distillation equipment, some of it imported from Germany.

Vodka production, however, was then disrupted by World War One, during which Rajamäki was reduced to producing only industrial products such as ether, which was used as an anesthetic. During

A painting of the Rajamäki distillery in Finland, dating back to the 1930s.

prohibition, which was introduced in Finland in 1919 and lasted until 1932, its main output was of alcohol-based toiletries.

The 1930s, however, saw a period of expansion and modernization at Rajamäki, by then renamed the State Alcohol Center after its nationalization in 1920. A new distillery came on stream on the site in 1935 and a completely new plant was commissioned in 1937.

During World War Two vodka production was again reduced and the plant was used to produce alcohol-based anti-tank "Molotov cocktails" and then pure alcohol that was used in the manufacture of motor fuel for army vehicles.

Distillation of vodka started again after the war and, after further expansion starting in the late 1940s, Rajamäki began to produce spirits on a regular basis in 1952. The next three decades saw enormous investment by the state and the Finnish vodka industry transformed itself into one of the most advanced distilling industries in the world. In 1975 a new bottling hall was built at Rajamäki and technology developed there and at the Koskenkorva distillery in the northwest of the country has been exported to several countries, including Scotland, Korea, and India.

Rationalization, however, came in the late 1980s. Because of its location close to the country's grain belt, distillation was concentrated in Koskenkorva and it is the only vodka distillery operating in the country

BELOW A panoramic view of Rajamäki today. Since the 1880s this town, 29 miles from Helsinki, has been the heart of vodka production in Finland.

today. Rajamäki remains one of the oldest working distilleries in the Western world, but its output is now sadly reduced to industrial alcohol and some spiced spirits such as Finnish gin. It also dilutes, bottles, and ships the vodka distilled at Koskenkorva.

Finland produces several brands of vodka but its reputation as a high-quality producer rests on two leading brands. Koskenkorva Viina (the word is the Finnish for *brännvin* or "burned wine"), a vodka with a small amount of sugar added to give it a smoother finish, was launched on the Finnish market in 1953. Koskenkorva Vodka, a clear and pure vodka, followed in 1952 and has become the leading brand on the Finnish market. Finlandia, a premium brand targeted primarily at export markets and now widely available around the world, was launched in 1970. Close to four million cases of the two brands are currently being sold a year, making Finland one of the most important vodka producers in the world today.

Finlandia is one of Finland's leading brands, targeted primarily at export markets.

Sweden

The shape of the Absolut bottle is based on the old-style Swedish medicine bottle.
Absolut was launched in 1871 by Lars Olsen Smith.

The distillation of *brännvin*, literally "burned wine," began in Sweden sometime in the fifteenth century. In the early years the spirit was made from imported wine rather than grain and was, therefore, a luxury. Its main social purpose was medicinal. It was also an important ingredient in the production of gunpowder and the authorities were quick to see the threat that consumption could have on the supply to powder makers: to keep control of the situation Stockholm's City Council threatened in 1476 to confiscate the spirit and equipment of anybody selling spirit without a license.

By the sixteenth century it was widely available in the streets of Stockholm as an intoxicating liquor but it remained a luxury until the following century. Then a switch to the use of grain rather than wine as a base, coupled with improvements in distilling techniques, made it far more accessible to the general populace. By the seventeenth century it had become the national drink, and production had radiated from the cities to the countryside.

In the same century the first tax on the spirit was introduced, during the regency of Queen Kristina, who also granted the exclusive right to sell beer, wine, and *brännvin* within a six-mile radius to innkeepers. The number of taverns flourished and so too did consumption, which was soon reaching dangerous levels. "Both soldiers and farmers are drawn to drinking *brännvin* and in this way consume their health and welfare and neglect both culture and service," says a report from the governor of northern Sweden in 1683.

Against a background of simmering opposition from farmers, prohibitions on the distillation of spirits were periodically imposed and then lifted when the opposition grew too strong. In 1775 King Gustav III even tried to impose a state system of crown distilleries, but illicit home distilling proceeded to grow to such an extent that the initiative was abandoned in 1787.

In the meantime distillation technology was improving steadily. Potatoes, a cheaper raw material than wheat at the time, were first used in distillation in the 1790s. During the following decade J. Fr. Dorn's

Distillation in an old Swedish farmhouse, 1830s. The Swedish Temperance Society banned home distilling in 1860.

composite still was introduced comprising a still, mash heater, rectifier, and condenser, which enabled distillers to obtain *brännvin* with an alcoholic strength of 120 proof using a single process. The real breakthrough, however, was Pictorius's dephlegmator with water-cooled pans, first used in Sweden in the 1820s. This enabled distillers to extract more impurities from the steam emerging from the still and produce vodka with a strength of 160 proof.

As a result of these developments, the country's output grew steadily, although the number of stills decreased. It is estimated that in 1756 there were 180,000 stills in Sweden, one for every 10 people. By the early 1870s this number had been reduced to about 3,481 and, over the next 10 years, to 564. Production over the same period, however, increased from around 51 million pints to almost 91 million pints.

Unfortunately, as production rose, so too did heavy drinking, and this led to the inevitable backlash. The Swedish Temperance Society was duly formed in 1837 and within 20 years had become such a strong political force that home distilling was at first restricted and then totally prohibited in 1860.

State control was also creeping into other aspects of the vodka business. The first *brännvin* company was formed in Falun in 1849 and in the same year was granted the exclusive right to serve and sell vodka through its restaurants. This was followed in 1865 by the formation of the Göteborg Utskänkningsaktiebolag, which enjoyed the same privilege in Göteborg, and by the Utskänkningsbolag in 1877, which was given the exclusivity for Stockholm. The aim of these companies was to promote sobriety, good morals, and better living conditions for the populace and for this reason their regulations were strict. For example, they closed promptly at 9 P.M., they did not serve serve anyone who was inebriated or under age, and vodka was served only with a meal. By 1905 the *brännvin* companies had become mandatory and 50 years

Lars Olsen Smith, a flamboyant figure in the history of the Swedish vodka industry.

later they were to be fused into one single nationwide retailing monopoly, the Systembolaget, which to this day remains in place.

Toward the end of the nineteenth century state control had come into collision with one of the most flamboyant figures to emerge from the Swedish vodka industry. Lars Olsson Smith controlled one-third of all vodka produced in Sweden before he learned to shave. In 1871 he installed a rectifier in his Reimersholm factory and six years later launched his Absolut Renadt Brännvin or Absolutely Pure Brännvin. When the Stockholm Utskänkningsbolag was formed he offered it his rectified vodka on condition that he would be its sole supplier. When it refused he declared war and opened his own shop on the island of Reimersholm. Drawn by the offer a free boat trip and enthused by the quality and low price of Smith's vodka, customers were soon flocking to his shop and the Utskänkningsbolag had to capitulate and accept his offer.

Smith was to have a further dust-up with the authorities and made and lost two fortunes before he died in 1913. But he was a man fighting against the tide of history. As the temperance movement grew in strength, so too did its political influence.

In 1910 the government assumed control of retailing of all alcoholic beverages and in 1914 it introduced a system of ration books, limiting the amount of vodka that any individual could purchase. In 1917 the state liquor company also purchased the largest rectifying company in the country and so brought production under state control. In the same year the Swedish Wine & Spirits Corporation (V&S) was formed,

The logo of The Swedish Wine & Spirit Corporation, Vin & Sprit.

thereby establishing a government monopoly on the manufacture, retailing, and import of all alcoholic beverages. In 1922 a public referendum narrowly voted against prohibition, but ration books were not abolished until 1955.

Today the national production monopoly is still in place and V&S has several distilleries across the country producing several brands of vodka, most of which are not exported. Sweden's reputation as a leading vodka producer, however, lies firmly on the shoulders of the Absolut brand, of which it sells nearly six million cases annually around the world. The production of the brand in the Åhus distillery in southern Sweden uses many of the methods first developed by Smith for his Absolut Renadt Brännvin, and a medal of the old "King of Vodka" is on every bottle in recognition of his contribution to the development of the Swedish vodka industry.

Western Europe

It is as difficult to trace the origins of vodka distillation in Western Europe as it is in the eastern half of the continent. Many countries have a long and illustrious tradition of distilling white spirits from a cereal base. But most of the European vodka brands that one sees on the market are comparatively recent developments and a response to the growth in popularity of the spirit in the 1960s, 1970s, and 1980s.

What is sure is that distillation came to the region as early as, if not earlier than, it did to Poland and Russia. Proof of this is that the remains of a still with a water cooling system dating back to the fourteenth century were discovered during excavations in Björkjaer in Denmark. As grain was probably the only material that these early distillers would have had at their disposal, it seems fair to surmise that the spirit they produced was not unlike what we know as vodka. By the fifteenth century, akvavit production was firmly established in Denmark. This was a white spirit flavoured with an infusion of herbs or other botanicals, which is very much what was being produced in eastern Europe at the time.

· Distillation was also known in the Netherlands from an early age. The Dutch claim that they were the first to distill wines from southwest France into an early form of brandy, and gin production, using wheat from the north of Holland, was firmly established by the end of the sixteenth century, when it was found by English soldiers who took it home to England enthusiastically. In 1679 the Russian Czar Peter I is said to have been so impressed with the quality of Dutch white spirit that he took the recipe back to Russia. In Germany, too, white spirits were being distilled—originally from wheat but later also from potatoes and molasses—in the sixteenth century.

The production of clear, unflavored vodka, sold as such and by this time a highly purified white spirit in the Eastern European style,

One of the original Royalty bottles. In Holland, blue is an aristocratic color.

Hero Jan Hooghoudt
appears on each
bottle.

probably did not take place until the nineteenth century. It was in 1888, for example, that Hero Jan Hooghoudt first began to distill his Royalty brand in Groningen in northern Holland, made from wheat and purified to an advanced degree. A further boost was to come from Russian émigrés fleeing the Russian revolution. The Wolfschmidts from Latvia distilled vodka in the Netherlands before emigrating to the United States. The Gorbatschows, a family of distillers from St Petersburg, set up their distillery in Berlin in 1921.

Most western European distillers, however, continued to focus on their national spirits such as akvavit and gin. It was not until vodka's popularity began to grow in the 1960s and 1970s that the big brands of the present day were launched. Furthermore, new brands continue to be launched on a regular basis and virtually every significant distilling company in Europe now has its own brand.

The comparatively short pedigree of most Western vodkas is unimportant. What is important is the centuries of experience of distilling white spirits and even whisky in the region, an experience that is being put to good use today. Gin, whisky, and akvavit distillers know a lot about distilling. They have access to high-quality grains and investment in distilling technology has been far higher than in the eastern half of the continent. The result is that many Western European vodka brands are of a very high quality.

As is the case in the United States purity, cleanliness, and smoothness are the main targets of Western European distillers. So most of the leading brands are comparatively neutral. They are, however, made from a variety of different raw materials—from wheat to molasses to potatoes —so there is a great deal of variety in the subtle differences between them, which is well worth investigating. And be warned: their quality also has a tendency to vary considerably.

Royalty vodka as it looks today.

The U.S.A.

The United States is today the second-largest vodka market in the world after Russia. Its vodka industry, however, is still in its infancy when compared with that of Russia or Poland. Vodka was first distilled in the country in the 1930s and it was not until about 30 years later that its popularity became established.

Vodka is said to have been first introduced to the United States by the Wolfschmidt company, which was founded in 1847 in Riga, the capital of Latvia. Before the Bolshevik revolution it was a supplier to the Czars, including Alexander III, but its owners, like all the other great Russian private distillers, were forced to flee by the new regime. They went first to the Netherlands, where the brand was produced for a while, and then to the United States. Today the Wolfschmidt brand is produced there and is owned by the huge American Brands Inc., of Jim Beam Bourbon fame.

Rudolph Kunett

Rudolph Kunett set up the country's first vodka distillery in 1934.

It was another Russian émigré, however, that has the best claim to be called the father of the American vodka industry. The Kunett family had been grain merchants in Russia before the revolution and one of their main customers had been the Smirnoffs, perhaps the leading Russian vodka producers at the turn of the century. Rudolph Kunett escaped the Bolshevik revolution and emigrated to the United States, where he became sales manager for the Helena Rubenstein cosmetics company.

In the early 1930s he visited Paris and met his old customer Vladimir Smirnoff, who had also fled the revolution and had put together enough money to start distilling again, albeit on a very much smaller scale than he had done during the company's heyday in Russia. Things were not going well. Believing that the American public would take to drinking vodka after prohibition, Kunett persuaded Smirnoff to sell him the secret formula for producing Smirnoff and the right to produce it in the United States. In 1934 he set up the country's first vodka distillery on the second floor of the Vaghi Woodwork Building in the center of Bethel, Connecticut, an area with sizeable Russian and Polish communities.

Kunett, however, was several decades before his time and his optimism was misplaced. At its peak the little company had eight employees and produced no more than six thousand cases of vodka a year. Most of it was under the Smirnoff brand but, with an eye on potential Polish customers, he also made some Zubrowka although it is unknown what process or materials he used. In 1939 Kunett sold the company to Heublein, a producer and distributor of wines, spirits and pre-mixed cocktails based in Hartford in the same state. Kunett got a job and $14,000.

Heublein was owned by an exceptional businessman, John G. Martin, and how he was persuaded to part with such a sum when no one in the United States knew about vodka—let alone drank it—remains a mystery. Nor were they to change their minds for another two decades. In the 1950s Martin did have some success. Together with his friend Jack Martin, who produced ginger beer and owned the Cock 'n' Bull restaurant in Los Angeles, he developed the Moscow Mule cocktail, which was originally served in a copper mug. And during the 1950s its popularity in cocktail bars grew impressively, driven by Martin's salesmanship and advertising nous. By the end of the decade other distillers had taken note of vodka's growing popularity and new brands, such as Gordon's, a vodka variant of the famous London dry gin, appeared.

Woody Allen advertising the Moscow Mule cocktail.

It was not until the 1960s, however, that a boom of unprecedented proportions was sparked off by a combination of vodka's mixability, a more relaxed lifestyle, and greater affluence. By 1975 Heublein was producing six million cases of vodka a year. Today it sells some 15 million cases of Smirnoff around the world and distills in several different countries, including Russia, its birthplace.

Other American and foreign distillers are also producing in large volume, many of them having set up production plants near the grain belt of the Midwest. McCormick Distillers produces just over one and a half million cases in Missouri, Barton Brands just over a million in Illinois. The Distillers Company, a subsidiary of the British United Distillers conglomerate, produces two million cases of Gordon's vodka at its plant at Plainfield, Illinois. From its base in Deerfield in the same state, American Brands produces over a million cases each of Wolfschmidt and Kamchatka. Its quality is based on two important factors: the use of some of the healthiest, high-grade grain in the world; and state-of-the-art distillation technology.

Vodka's great attraction in the United States, however, has always been its lack of aroma and taste, and it is this that makes it an ideal base for cocktails. Indeed these were the attributes that John Martin initially used to advertise Smirnoff, calling it a "white whisky" under the slogan "No taste. No smell."

American vodkas, therefore, are very different from their Russian and Polish counterparts. Do not expect much character in them as all the impurities of the raw spirit have either been burned or filtered off. Instead they should be judged on their purity, cleanliness, and neutrality. Smoothness too is an attribute that American distillers are interested in and some are a lot smoother than others. The best can, at a pinch, be drunk neat and cold. Most, however, are destined, by design, to go straight into the cocktail shaker.

Many production plants in the United States are near the grain belt of the Midwest, Barton brands produce just over a million cases per year in Illinois.

Flavored Vodkas

Colored vodka and a made-up girl are good for nothing.

—OLD POLISH PROVERB

The practice of flavoring vodka has been going on for centuries.

The production of flavored vodkas is a practice probably as old as the distillation of the spirit itself. Vodka, like most other spirits, started life as a medicine rather than as a pleasurable drink. So most early vodkas were infused with medicinal herbs and spices and were kept in the medicine cabinet.

The practice of flavoring, however, continued even after vodka started to be drunk for enjoyment. Other additives with no medicinal properties, such as berries, pepper, and even tobacco, began to be used, and it is easy to understand why. Early distillation methods were, at best, rudimentary. The spirit was distilled only once and, despite heroic efforts at filtration, was probably highly contaminated with impurities. Aromatic additives were the only way of making the first vodkas at all palatable.

Flavoring vodka, however, was to become a great tradition in countries like Poland and Russia, particularly after the right to distill was given to the gentry. These were wealthy folk producing spirits for

Cherry Wiśniówka is Poland's favorite cherry vodka and is a beautiful deep color.

their own consumption and that of their household and guests, so no expense was spared. They had the produce of their own estates at hand, such as fruits and berries, and they could afford to buy spices imported from abroad. They flavored their vodkas with prime materials and developed their own formulas, which were passed down from one generation to another. And some of the great flavored vodkas produced in Eastern Europe today are undoubtedly derived from this tradition.

Modern flavored vodkas, however, are produced on an industrial scale. Such is their popularity that few brands do not have flavored varieties and a new technology for their production has had to be developed.

Citrus fruits such as lime make good flavorings.

Most producers are unwilling to reveal the exact formula they use for flavoring, except to claim that all the ingredients they use are natural (most countries have strict regulations on the use of artificial additives in vodka anyway). This may be the case, but the preparation of these ingredients is a highly complicated process.

The major problem is that flavoring ingredients such as fruit can contain elements that inevitably lead to discoloration and unpleasant aromas and tastes. Fresh fruit, for example, contains pectin, acids, and solids that can make a vodka cloudy, brownish, and bitter. The challenge to the producer is to get rid of these and add only the elements that will give pleasant fruity aromas and flavors. Most of them buy in natural essences, concentrates, and clear oils extracted from the skins and add these to the vodka after distillation. They also tend to add these ingredients from more than just one fruit. Most of the ingredients added to a lemon-flavored vodka, for example, will be extracted from lemons.

Try making your own lemon-flavored vodka.

But there will be others extracted from different fruits, most probably limes, to enhance or complement the flavors of the base fruit.

It all sounds very impressive. But does it really work?

My own opinion is that the technology still has some way to go. In the case of citrus fruits the technology appears well advanced and there are some very good lemon, lime, and orange vodkas available. This, however, is not always the case with other popular flavorings. Some blackcurrant vodkas do smell genuine enough but taste totally artificial and unpleasant.

Furthermore, I see no point in buying a vodka that has been flavored with a type of fruit that is readily available. If you want a lemon-flavored vodka, then why not add a squeeze of fresh lemon juice? If you want a peach-flavored one, then steep the peaches in vodka for a few days. Because it is done on a small scale and because, presumably, you will be consuming it reasonably quickly, flavoring your own vodka is not difficult.

Where I believe flavored vodkas really come into their own is when they are made with products that are difficult to find, or follow a complicated formula. Some of the flavored vodkas from Eastern Europe in particular draw from their great heritage and are impossible to reproduce. There are several of these listed in the directory. Jarzębiak from Poland, which is flavored with rowanberries, is a good example. Or the Russian Okhotnichya, the Hunter's Vodka as it is known, which is flavored with 11 ingredients including ginger, juniper, tormentil, and ashweed roots and has some white port-style wine added to give it sweetness.

These are very distinctive powerful-tasting vodkas, made to be drunk chilled and straight. They may not be to everyone's taste and, in some cases, the quality of the base vodka is not what it should be. But at least they are different. And, when drinking them, you get the feeling that you are drinking something with a real heritage that has been around and appreciated for generations.

Jarzębiak, which comes from Poland, is flavored with rowanberries.

FLAVORING YOUR OWN VODKA

If you are interested in flavored vodkas why not try and flavor your own? It is not an expensive or complicated process and it is great fun.

Start with something simple. If you like peaches, peel a couple that are good and ripe (do not use canned ones) and cut them into chunks. Put these into a clean bottle and pour in the vodka. You will have to experiment with the quantities of the ingredients used but I would suggest two peaches per ordinary 28 or 29 fl. oz. bottle, more if you want a stronger flavor. Within three or four days the vodka will be infused with the peach flavor, so strain it through a clean cloth if you do not like the solids and you have a much better peach-flavored vodka than those produced commercially. The same can be done with other sweet fruits such as pineapple. Alternatively, if you like hot vodkas, put some well-washed, whole chiles into a bottle and fill it up with vodka, but you will have to leave for a little bit longer.

For something a little more sophisticated here are some suggestions from William Pokhlebkin, who claims that these give you a genuine taste of the flavored vodkas produced during the "golden age" of vodka in eighteenth-century Russia.

Get a good-quality, clear vodka (Pokhlebkin, of course, insists that it must be Russian). Then buy some lemon and bitter orange peel and some St. John's wort (a type of herb). Put a small quantity (more if you wish to get a really dark color) of the peels and the herb into three separate bottles, seal them, and leave them to steep for a week to ten days.

The result is three bright and clear vodkas but with startlingly different colors. The St John's wort gives the vodka a pale green color, the lemon peel turns the vodka yellow, and the orange imparts almost a crimson hue. "On a table served with snacks they will form a unique and sparklingly brilliant still-life to appease the most exacting artistic taste," Pokhlebkin then concludes. "Speaking of the flavor and taste of these liquors, they can only be truly appreciated personally, for no words in any language, even native Russian, can do that better."

Fruit accounts for a wide range of flavored vodkas.

How to Serve and Drink Vodka

For most Westerners vodka is a tasteless, neutral spirit used as a base for cocktails or to be mixed with juices or other mixers. In Eastern Europe and the Nordic countries they know better. Vodka is drunk neat, usually ice-chilled, and in a small glass. It is also often drunk as an accompaniment to food.

Perhaps this is because Eastern vodkas tend to have more flavor than those produced in the West, where the distiller's main aims are purity, cleanliness, and neutrality. Some of the best Western vodkas, however, do merit being drunk neat simply because they are of such a high quality. An ice-chilled Fris (which is made to be drunk when nearly frozen), or a Royalty or a Sterling is a wonderful spirit.

Frïs Skandia is made to be drunk when nearly frozen. Western vodkas merit being drunk neat because they are of such a high quality.

If you want to taste a vodka clinically get a glass that curves inwards at the mouth to retain the aromas, and perform the test I suggest on p.55. Any impurities will soon become apparent. Odors such as that of boiled cabbage, toffee, or stock cubes are often released by vodkas that have been badly distilled (see panel on page 56). Look out too for hints of lemon or other citrus fruits. Essences from these are sometimes used in small quantities to mask unpleasant odors arising from poor distillation or rectification.

If this process seems too clinical, particularly if you are only going to drink vodka as a mixer, do not forget that more vodka is produced in the world than any other spirit. And not surprisingly, there are many brands, even well-known brands, that are not made as well as they should be, usually because the distiller is cutting corners somewhere to save money. There is no longer any excuse for this. Distillation technology has progressed too far.

If you are drinking for pleasure, the right type of glass is essential. Small, stemless shot glasses are popular and are easy to chill in the freezer, but they have the disadvantage that your hand warms up the spirit. It is better, therefore, to use clear glasses that have a stem and contain about 3.3 fluid ounces. In Russia they tend to use long, thin glasses not unlike a slender champagne flute, called *stopkis*. In Poland they go for smaller, more rounded ones like small goblets. They also tend to serve vodka from a small, transparent decanter rather than from the bottle. Do not fill these glasses to the brim. Just fill them about two-thirds full.

Chill these glasses in the freezer so that they frost over when you take them out and do the same with the decanter or the bottle. Many vodkas freeze solid if left in the freezer for too long so don't overdo it, just get it very well chilled. The low temperature will, at first, suppress some of the more delicate aromas. But these will slowly begin to reveal themselves as you drink, so make sure that you continue to nose it each time you take a sip, the way you would with a wine. Smelling and tasting the unfolding of aroma and flavor in the glass of good vodka is one of the greatest pleasures of drinking it.

It is also well worth looking at the vodka before tasting or nosing it. It should be bright and crystal clear with no signs of opaqueness or discoloring. Some will be thicker, more viscous and dense than others, particularly those from Eastern Europe. This indicates that they have either some fusel oil left in or have had something like glycerine added to give them a bigger "mouth feel" and they will be more oily and thicker in the mouth. This is often done to counter the slight harshness of the alcohol.

TASTING VODKA

1 Nose the vodka carefully before and during tasting it.

2 Take a small sip and roll it over your tongue, releasing its tastes.

3 Draw some air over it, in order to release its flavors and aromas.

4 Swallow and assess the "finish"— how long flavors stay in the mouth.

IMPURITIES

These are the impurities most frequently found in a poorly distilled vodka with a guide to their odors.

Acrolein	sharp, acrid and pungent.
B	meaty, like a stock cube.
DMTs	cooked cabbage or drains.
Esters	sweet and fruity.
Feints	amyl alcohol, like thinned-down nail-enamel remover.
Acetal	green-skin apples.
Diacetyl	sweet, buttery, or toffeeish.
Methyl thiazole	catty, very unpleasant.
Ionone	perfumed, heavy, sweet.

ALCOHOLIC STRENGTH

In America the proof system is still operational. For example, 100 proof is equivalent to 50% alcoholic volume and 80 proof to 40%. The proof system was originally tested by putting a lit match to a mixture of the spirits with gunpowder. If it ignited then the whisky was of sufficient strength and "proved." The gunpowder would not flash if the spirit was too weak. In Europe alcohol is measured by percentage volume at 5°F.

INFORMATION BOXES

THE SPIRIT FACTS BOXES in this Directory give the name of the brand owner, the location of the distillery or rectification plant, an estimate of annual production and sales, and the different strengths at which it is bottled. Don't forget that many brand owners don't do their own distillation or rectification, in which case no distillery location has been given.

THE RATING BOXES offer my own personal assessment of the sample bottle supplied by the brand owners for tasting during the long period of this book's compilation. The star system denotes the following assessments:

★★★★ Outstanding   ★★★ Very Good   ★★ Good   ★ Acceptable

Those brands that have not been awarded any stars and have been classified as "not graded" are those in which I found evidence of poor distillation or rectification.

PART TWO

THE
VODKA
DIRECTORY

THE WEST

There are more Western vodka brands listed in this directory than from either Russia or Poland. In fact there are 39 altogether, with examples from most countries in Western Europe, the Nordic countries and the United States.

What is fascinating about them is that their quality varies enormously. Some are truly outstanding while others are, quite frankly, dreadful. So what is an outstanding Western vodka?

The ideal Western vodka is one that has been distilled, rectified, and filtered to the highest possible level of purity. This means that it should have no "off" aromas or smells, just perhaps a bit of the aroma of ethyl alcohol. It should also be light and crisp without the slightly oily, heavy texture that is often found in vodkas from Poland and Russia. It should also be very, very smooth. If all this is achieved then you have an ideal

Lake shore, Liesjarvi, Finland. The quality of vodka produced in the West – Western Europe, the Nordic countries, and the United States – varies enormously. The ideal Western vodka is very pure.

spirit to enhance a cocktail or give some bite to a mixer such as a tonic or a fruit juice. Very few Western vodkas achieve this high level of excellence but those that do are excellent spirits which can be a delight to drink even on their own.

Western vodka, however, is a controversial spirit. Ask any distiller in Russia or Poland what he thinks of it and words such as "uninteresting" and "boring" are bound to crop up. And this is an opinion that has been shared by many journalists and writers in the West who, accustomed to writing about other, more characterful spirits like rum, Scotch, and Cognac, have had few good words to say about it.

This, I believe, is a little unfair. Western vodka is a very different product from its Eastern counterpart and Western distillers are trying to achieve a totally different goal than those of the East.

In this section I have looked at the vodkas and rated them using totally different criteria, looking primarily for purity, lightness, and smoothness. As this is what their producers are aiming for, I think that it is the only way to judge them.

Absolut

SPIRIT FACTS

Owner V&S Vin & Sprit
Distillery Åhus, Sweden
Production 5 million cases
Strengths Absolut Blue 80 proof
Absolut Red 100 proof
Absolut Citron 80 proof
Absolut Kurant 80 proof
Absolut Peppar 80 proof

The story of how Lars Olsson Smith shook up the Swedish vodka industry and produced the first "Absolut Renadt Brännvin"—or Absolute Pure Vodka—is told in another chapter. His was a technological revolution, enabling him to rectify his vodka to an unprecedented level of purity in Sweden. A century later his vodka was used as the basis for another revolution, but this time one that had as much to do with packaging and marketing as it did with production technology.

It was in the 1970s that the surge of vodka consumption in the United States persuaded the Swedish vodka-producing monopoly Vin & Sprit (V&S) to develop a new vodka

RATING

Absolut
★★

Absolut Citron
★

Absolut Kurant
not graded

Absolut Peppar
★★★★

especially for that market, one of premium quality that would reflect the long tradition of vodka distillation in Sweden.

With little experience of either exporting, advertising, or packaging the president of V & S, Lars Lindmark, set up a marketing team to develop the brand, which called in American experts to help. At first they played with concepts that would reflect the Swedish origins of the brand. Prototype products such as "Royal Court Vodka" in a frosted carafe and "Swedish Blond Vodka" depicting pillaging Vikings were produced, but all were eventually rejected.

The breakthrough came when one of the team found an old medicine bottle in an antique shop in Stockholm's old quarter, which gave them the basic shape that they needed. Subsequently it was

TASTING NOTES

ABSOLUT BLUE

Very neutral on the nose with just a touch of cereal aroma and a hint of alcohol. Very good mouth feel, dryish in style but with some very light hints of caramelization. Just touches of needle from the alcohol. Sweetish but rather short on the finish.

I maintain that this makes one of the finest vodka tonics in the world, perhaps because the mouth feel of the vodka lends a bit more weight to the mixture than other, lighter vodkas. Alternatively, put it in the freezer to drink ice-chilled when it becomes thick in texture, smooth, and very dry.

ABSOLUT CITRON

I am not persuaded by the aroma of this vodka, which is light and concentrated but one-dimensional and, to me, a bit artificial. A bit bitter on the palate but with a penetrating citrus flavor that cannot quite disguise some impurities in the base spirit. Some alcohol burn. Persistent citrus flavor on the finish. Use as a mixer.

decided not to use a label, so that the vodka's clarity could be appreciated and to use blue and black lettering on the glass.

The name, too, caused problems. Initially the team thought of calling it "Absolute Pure Vodka" but found that the word "pure" could not be used on the label of an alcoholic beverage and that "absolute," being an adjective, could not be used as a trademark in the United States. Eventually the brand name was reduced to Absolut and the words "Country of Sweden" added to give a Scandinavian impression of purity and cleanliness. The final touch was the Lars Olsson Smith medallion, in order to add a sense of tradition.

The first consignment of Absolut left the Åhus distillery for Boston early in 1979. Fired by what is generally regarded as some of the most innovative and witty advertising ever produced for a spirit, sales of the brand went through the roof. Today Absolut Blue and Absolut Citron are the two largest-imported vodkas on the US market and the whole range sells more than five million cases a year around the world.

Its sales success, however, tells only half the story. More than any other brand since Smirnoff's huge success in the 1950s and 1960s, it was Absolut that helped to change the West's conception of vodka. Suddenly it got a new injection of cachet and fashionableness. The packaging of the product, its advertising all became as important as its quality. You will find that most vodkas in the West today are more innovatively packaged than any other spirit.

Absolut is produced in the Åhus distillery in southern Sweden, which first became operational in 1906. Local grain is used in the production and the initial raw spirit is distilled to a strength of 170–180 proof in continuous stills. It is then rectified through a four-column apparatus from which it emerges at a strength of

190 proof and is diluted to 80 proof using treated water from the distillery's own wells. The bottles are all made in the nearby Limmared glassworks, which first opened in 1741 and produced the original medicine bottle on which Absolut's bottle design is based.

When I first tasted Absolut on the terrace of a café in the old quarter of Stockholm I was persuaded that it was one of the world's greatest vodkas and that it made an outstanding vodka tonic. Since then some of my friends in the industry have criticized the brand, suggesting that its enormous worldwide success has led to its being churned out just a bit too quickly. Certainly, in the sample used for these tasting notes, the vodka did show some faults, touches of caramelization in particular. But my faith in the brand and in its production process remains unshaken. I am less convinced by the flavored versions.

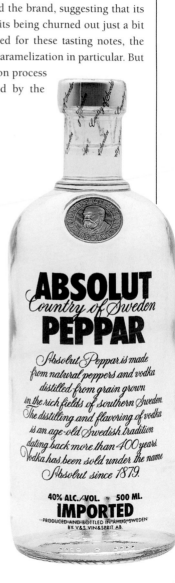

TASTING NOTES

ABSOLUT KURANT

I think this has improved since I first tasted it a couple of years ago but I still find the aroma a bit artificial and a bit reminiscent of bubble gum. Sweet and cloying on the palate, artificial in flavor, and with aggressive alcohol burn. Leaves a bitter-sweet aftertaste in the mouth. I find this an incongruous member of the Absolut stable.

ABSOLUT PEPPAR

This has an amazing and very distinctive bouquet of Mexican Jalapeño chiles. Thickish in texture, very smooth with an initial sensation of sweetness. This does linger on the palate but then the fire lights up, pushing it into the background. The fire continues for quite a time on the tongue—and some people will find it a bit hot.

This is a fascinating vodka, very well flavored. I have given it a high rating, which some people will disagree with, but I was, after all, born in Mexico!

Aslanov

SPIRIT FACTS

Owner Distillers Bruggeman

Distillery Ghent, Belgium

Production figures not available

Strengths Aslanov Vodka 80, 92 proof
Aslanov Lemon 80 proof
Aslanov Blackcurrant 80 proof

Michael and Nina Aslanian were originally from Rostov-on-the-Don, the great port near the Sea of Azov in southern Russia. Like many of their compatriots, however, they were forced to flee from their country in 1917 during the Russian Revolution and they eventually settled in Brussels, where they started to produce vodka again. Initially their customers were fellow homesick émigrés, but soon native Belgians also began to appreciate their vodka.

The brand was bought by Distillers Bruggeman in 1979, a company founded in 1884 when Pieter Bruggeman first started distilling jenevers and fruit liqueurs in a distillery in the Flemish city of Ghent.

The company has a state-of-the-art and ecologically friendly rectification facility in the same city and buys in raw spirit at 192 proof which is submitted to strict quality control by the company's technical department. It is then rectified and diluted to

RATING

Aslanov Vodka
★★

Aslanov Blackcurrant
★★

Aslanov Lemon
★★

the required strength. The flavored versions are made by macerating the fruit in alcohol for several days and then distilling the spirit in a pot still to give the final product more intensity and honesty of aroma and taste.

This is a sound range of vodkas and it has won several awards at the International Wine and Spirits Competition in London. The 80 proof version of the clear vodka won a silver medal in 1995 and the Blackcurrant and Lemon flavors did the same in 1996.

TASTING NOTES

ASLANOV VODKA

Very neutral on the nose with just faint, very faint, touches of caramel. Quite soft and smooth on the palate but a bit of burn develops in the stronger 92 proof version version because of the extra alcohol. Slightly caramelized but not unpleasantly so. Nice, long aftertaste in which the toffee comes slightly more to the fore.

ASLANOV BLACKCURRANT

Very intense, pungent, and concentrated blackcurrant aromas. The intensity, however, tends to fade a little on the palate. Smooth, very pleasant but quite spirity. This is a well-made flavored vodka that will appeal to those who like strongly flavored vodkas.

ASLANOV LEMON

Again, this has a wonderfully honest citrus aroma with, I believe, a touch of lime. On the palate, well balanced with plenty of citrus flavor and a delicious touch of lemon on the finish. Makes a delightfully crisp vodka tonic.

Barclay's

SPIRIT FACTS

Owner Barton Brands

Distilleries Bardstown, Kentucky; Los Angeles, California; Atlanta, Georgia

Production figures not available

Strength 80 proof

Owned for many years by the Canadian company Hiram Walker, this brand was bought by Barton Brands in 1988 and was followed into the stable one year later by its sister brand, Crystal Palace.

RATING

Barclay's

★★

The vodka is made from neutral grain spirit, which is rectified in one of Barton's three plants in Kentucky, California, and Georgia. It is then charcoal-filtered, which accounts for its clean, pure, and neutral character.

This is not a particularly exciting vodka, but it is honest and well made with no pretensions. Would score more highly if it was a little bit smoother.

TASTING NOTES

BARCLAY'S

Nice, very clean and pure nose, just slightly spirity. Very clean in taste and slightly sweet in style, reasonably smooth but a bit mouth-puckeringly astringent and with a little fire. Quite sweet and persistent on the finish. Apart from the slight astringency, one of the better US vodkas featured in this book.

Drink as a mixer.

Barton

SPIRIT FACTS

Owner Barton Brands
Rectification plants Bardstown, Kentucky;
Los Angeles,
California; Atlanta, Georgia
Production 1.19 million cases
Strengths 80, 100 proof

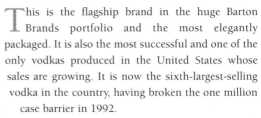

This is the flagship brand in the huge Barton Brands portfolio and the most elegantly packaged. It is also the most successful and one of the only vodkas produced in the United States whose sales are growing. It is now the sixth-largest-selling vodka in the country, having broken the one million case barrier in 1992.

The company first came into the limelight when it was taken over by Ellis Goodman's Amalgamated Distilled Products in 1982. Subsequently, Amalgamated merged with Argyll Foods and, in 1987, Goodman led a management buy-out of the Barton division and set off on an ambitious spending spree. The Barclay's brand was acquired in 1988 and Crystal Palace in the following year. Then in 1995 the company bought United Distillers-Glenmore from the British giant United Distillers, of Johnnie Walker and Gordon's gin fame, bringing another six well-known brands into the fold. Today Goodman is still very much in control of the company and Barton is the second-largest supplier of vodka in the United States, selling over 3.5 million cases.

RATING

Barton
★

Barton, Barton Brands' flagship brand, is the most elegantly packaged.

The company is unwilling to discuss its production process but Barton vodka is distilled in the company's three production plants in Kentucky, California, and Georgia. Made entirely from high-quality American grain, the vodka is then filtered through charcoal for extra purity. The result is a very neutral, very Western vodka to use as a mixer.

Barton vodka is part of a brand range that also includes a Barton "London" dry gin and a Bourbon.

The tasting notes are for the lighter 80 proof version.

TASTING NOTES

BARTON VODKA

Very, very light and neutral bouquet with a light aroma of toffee in the background. Slightly sweet and cloying in the mouth with touches of caramelization and a bit of needle. Lingers well in the mouth.

Black Death

SPIRIT FACTS

Owner Richmond Distillers
Distillery Warrington, UK
Production figures not available
Strength 80 proof

This is one of the few humorously packaged vodka brands in the world, but do we really want to have a top-hatted skull grinning at us from the label when we are drinking a vodka? First launched by the Sigurdsson family from Iceland (who probably got the idea from the Icelandic schnapps Islenskt Brennivín, nicknamed Black Death because of its lurid, black label) the brand has become very successful in recent years. It acquired greater dynamism when bought by the Luxemburg-based company Richmond Distillers, which is partly owned by the British distiller G. & J. Greenall.

RATING

Black Death
not graded

No one could tell me what this vodka is made from, but I rather suspect it is molasses. The raw spirit is bought from outside sources and is then rectified at Greenall's famous Warrington plant in Cheshire. The vodka is then filtered through carbon filters.

TASTING NOTES

BLACK DEATH

Almost totally odorless but with just some hints of sweetness in the background. Very sweet and cloying on the palate with strong taste of burned sugars, but very smooth with hardly a trace of needle. Very strong flavor of toffee on the finish. Definitely a mixer.

Blavod

SPIRIT FACTS

Owner The Original Black Vodka Company
Distilleries several in the UK
Production figures not available
Strength 80 proof

When this brand was first launched in the fall of 1996 I phoned up its producer, the Original Black Vodka Company, and asked the obvious question: Why black? "Why *should* vodka be clear?" asked an enthusiastic spokesman. "Wouldn't it be more interesting, exciting, alluring, mysterious, sexier if it was black? We're out to change people's preconceptions about vodka." So, if you are a vodka traditionalist, this is not a brand for you.

The company has the vodka prepared and bottled for it by Heyman Distillers, a company created by former members of the production team at James Burrough Ltd, which distills the famous Beefeater gin in the old Kennington distillery in South London. Led by Charles Heyman, a member of the Burrough family, they set up on their own when the company was sold to the British brewer Whitbread in the 1980s and they now specialize in the blending and bottling of white spirits for trade buyers. There is, therefore, a considerable amount of expertise behind the brand, although quite how Blavod is produced is obviously a closely guarded secret.

RATING

Blavod
★★

This is a very unusual vodka and for more reasons than just its color. Something, perhaps several flavorings have been added, but I have no idea what they are. It is not a vodka for purists but I personally quite like it.

TASTING NOTES

BLAVOD

Hold this vodka up to the light in a tall thin glass and the color is not black but more of an inky blue-gray. On the nose it is so neutral as to be almost odorless. Good mouth feel with a light sweetness and a medicinal, slightly herbal flavor that lingers in the mouth long after the vodka has been swallowed. There is a trace of needle.

Try it neat and slightly chilled. Alternatively, add just a touch of Noilly Prat to make a black Vodka Martini. This gives it some aroma and, on the palate, it becomes complex with the medicinal, herbal qualities of the vodka mixing with the sweet oakiness of the vermouth. Like the vodka itself, it will not be to everyone's taste. But this vodka is trying to be different and it certainly produces a very different Martini.

Cossack

SPIRIT FACTS

Owner United Distillers
Distillery Laindon, England
Production figures not available
Strength 75 proof

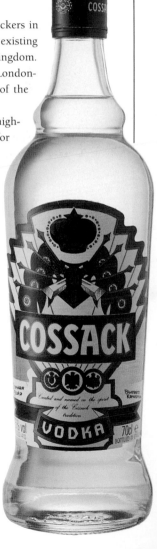

First produced by the gin producer J.J. Vickers in the 1960s, this is probably the oldest existing vodka brand to be produced in the United Kingdom. Vickers was then taken over by another London-based gin distiller, Booth's, and is now part of the giant United Distillers group.

The company buys in carefully chosen, high-quality, neutral spirit made from molasses for this brand, which accounts for its slightly sweet character. Then it is charcoal-filtered and bottled in Essex, England, at its distillation plant.

RATING

Cossack
★★

This is a good vodka but the brand has gone into sad decline in recent years. Once, it was a powerful player in the U.K. vodka market, but its sales are now more or less confined to Northern Ireland.

TASTING NOTES

COSSACK

Very, very neutral on the nose with just touches of alcohol and sweetness emanating from the molasses base. Sweetish and rich in style but very clean and pure with good smoothness and only a touch of needle. Sweet with slight traces of citrus flavor on the finish. Quite persistent.
Use as a mixer or in cocktails.

Cristalnaya

SPIRIT FACTS

Owner Richmond Distillers
Distillery Warrington, England
Production figures not available
Strength 80 proof

This is the third brand that has been produced by the Luxembourg-based Richmond Distillers in association with G. & J. Greenall, which is the company's major shareholder. Greenall has been distilling white spirits in England since 1761 and initially made its name in the vodka market with the high-profile Vladivar brand before selling it to the Whyte & Mackay group in 1990.

RATING
Cristalnaya Special
★★

As is the case with Black Death and Selekt, the two other brands in the company's portfolio, Cristalnaya is produced at Greenall's production facility in Warrington, Cheshire, England. Raw alcohol is brought in from outside suppliers and is then rectified to a high level of purity and carbon-filtered. The result is a good, middle-of-the-road Western brand that is ideal for mixing or to use as a base for cocktails. Most of its sales, however, are in Russia and the other countries of the CIS.

TASTING NOTES

CRISTALNAYA SPECIAL

Very, very neutral in aroma, almost odorless with just a faint trace of alcohol. Sweetish and rich in style but with no traces of caramelization, very clean and with a little needle. Just a light touch of toffee flavor on the rather short finish.

Crystal Palace

SPIRIT FACTS

Owner Barton Brands

Rectification plants Bardstown, Kentucky;
Los Angeles, California; Atlanta, Georgia

Production figures not available

Strength 80 proof

This is one of the core vodka brands in the Barton Brands range acquired from the giant Hiram Walker in 1989. Its sales have been growing in recent years and have helped Barton to become the second-largest supplier of vodka to the U.S. market with sales of 3.5 million cases. Crystal Palace is now the seventeenth-largest-selling vodka brand in the United States.

The vodka is produced from 100 percent grain and is rectified in the company's three plants in Kentucky, California, and Georgia.

This is an accessibly priced brand with distribution more or less limited to the United States. Very neutral in character.

TASTING NOTES

CRYSTAL PALACE

Odorless, very clean bouquet with just a trace of alcohol. Mouth-puckering, drying your gums and tongue, but at the same time quite rich and sweet. Very clean in taste with no evident impurities. Quite persistent finish with some fire.

RATING

Crystal Palace
★

Czarina

SPIRIT FACTS

Owner Barton Brands
Rectification plants Bardstown, Kentucky;
Los Angeles,
California; Atlanta, Georgia
Production figures not available
Strength 80 proof

Despite the Russian name and the double-headed imperial eagle on the label, this is an American vodka that has been produced for many years by the giant Barton Brands, producers of Barclay's, Barton, Crystal Palace, Fleischmann's, Mr Boston and Schenley, in its distilleries in California, Georgia, and Kentucky. The company is unwilling to give much information about the production process used except to say that it is made from American grain.

This is a popularly priced vodka, rather tackily packaged in a lightweight bottle that feels rather like perspex. Czarina is undoubtedly a mixer.

RATING

Czarina
not graded

TASTING NOTES

CZARINA

The bouquet of this vodka is so light and neutral as to be almost nonexistent. Just a light touch of alcohol in the background. Heavy alcohol burn in the mouth with touches of sweetness and sourness.
This is not my favorite vodka and I know that Barton can do better.

Danzka

SPIRIT FACTS

Owner Danisco Distillers
Distillery Aalborg, Denmark
Production figures not available
Strengths all versions 80 proof

This is Denmark's premier vodka brand, first produced in the 1980s by Thomas Anton, a small but enterprising akvavit producer who saw an opening for a cleverly packaged Danish vodka on the booming world market. Its historical pedigree, therefore, is short, but it is now owned by the giant Danisco Distillers which has been distilling white spirits for akvavit for over 150 years in its historic Aalborg distillery in Northern Jutland. The company bought the brand in 1994 and its quality is now much improved.

The Aalborg distillery was first opened in 1846 by Isidor Henius, who wanted to make a superior-quality akvavit. Soon afterwards he introduced column rectification into his distillery and became the first Danish distiller to be able to describe his spirit as "rectified, filtered, fusel-free." In 1881, however, the distillery was taken over by the industrialist C.E. Tietgen, who bought several distilling companies in Denmark and formed the giant De Danske Spritfabrikker or Danish Distillers. Such was the quality of the spirits he produced

RATING

Danzka Vodka
★★★

Danzka Citron
★★★

Danzka Currant
★★★

that, toward the end of the century, Czar Peter ordered the Russian ambassador in Copenhagen to get the recipe.

In 1989 the company merged with several other companies in one of the biggest mergers in Danish commercial history to form Danisco A/S. Today the company is the only producer of spirits in Denmark with distilleries in Aalborg and Grena, both in Jutland, and supplies a number of other spirit producers both in Denmark and abroad.

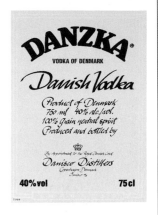

Danzka vodka is made from high-quality Danish grain with a high proportion of wheat which

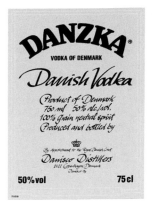

is crushed and cooked under pressure to break down the starch. After fermentation the wash passes through a continuous six-column distillation and rectification process and is diluted with water that has been demineralized by ion-exchange treatment. It is then carbon-filtered three times. For the flavored versions flavorings from natural ingredients are added to the vodka after filtration.

This is an innovatively packaged range of vodkas advertised under the slogan "Vodka on Metal." I like the style of the flavored vodkas; they are less pungent and more subtle than many of their competitors with a delicacy and honesty of flavor and aroma that I find very attractive. The unflavored version is a pleasure to drink and is what one would expect from a company with centuries of distilling experience.

TASTING NOTES

DANZKA VODKA

So clean and neutral that it is difficult to get any bouquet at all. Smooth on the palate to begin with but just a bit of needle comes in toward the end. Quite rich in style with good mouth feel. Clean finish.
This is a lovely vodka very much in the Western style with few blemishes. Good enough to drink on its own.

DANZKA CITRON

Very, very light on the nose but with an honest aroma of lemon. Very soft, mellow lemon flavor in the mouth, nicely rounded and smooth. Short on the finish but nice and fragrant. If I were to look for a citrus vodka to drink chilled and neat, this is one that I would go for. Also good mixed with tonic.

DANZKA CURRANT

This smells gently of real blackcurrants with no hints of impurities. On the palate the blackcurrant flavor is almost in the background, providing a backdrop rather than the main taste sensation. The base vodka used is smooth enough but has been left with enough needle to prevent the fruit flavor from becoming too sweet. Fragrant, long-lasting finish.

1822

SPIRIT FACTS

Owner Boisset
Distillery Nuits St Georges, France
Production 2,500 cases
Strength all 75 proof

The town of Nuits St Georges in the heart of Burgundy's wine-growing region is an incongruous place to find the headquarters of a vodka-producing company. The firm of Morin, however, has been producing fruit liqueurs and cassis in the region for years and the launch of a range of flavored vodkas was seen as a natural extension to this activity.

The Morins first settled in Burgundy in the fifteenth century, but it was not until 1822 that Claude Morin opened a wine-and-spirits company in the town. Since then the company has firmly established itself as an important liqueur producer and is now part of the Boisset group of companies.

RATING

1822 Vodka
★★

1822 Citron
★

1822 Orange
★

1822 Rose
★★★

1822 Cola
not graded

The expertise in macerating fruit in spirit and extracting its aromas and flavors has been passed down from father to son across five generations of Morins and is now being put to good use in the vodka side of the business. The vodka brand was launched in 1995 and its innovative packaging, designed to look modern and distance the brand from the pseudo-Russian imagery that is the hallmark of so many other Western brands, has already won a design award in France, the Grand Prix de Design Strategie.

The company buys in alcohol from outside suppliers, but does the flavoring itself. Natural ingredients are macerated in spirit to produce essences of the different flavors, which are then added to the vodka after distillation. The products are then filtered and bottled in one-pint bottles in Nuits St Georges.

TASTING NOTES

1822 VODKA

The list of ingredients on the label (alcohol, water, natural extract) gives it away. This vodka has had a touch of citrus essence added to it as an enhancer but this is not unpleasant. Gentle, very light and pleasant citrus aroma. Very smooth on the palate, just slightly thick in texture and with a hint of lemon flavor. There is a bit of alcohol burn but not aggressive. Nice, medium weight finish with no needle.

I find this a very pleasant vodka, good enough to drink on its own.

1822 CITRON

Lovely, very intense aroma with scents of lemon and lime. Quite smooth with reasonably intense citrus flavor but just slightly bitter. Persistent, citrusy finish with a bit of fire. Makes a good mixer.

This is an unusual range of vodkas. Many other producers have launched lemon and orange versions, but who would have thought of a vodka with the scent of rose petals and "flavors reminiscent of an English country garden"? Or one flavored with cola but still bottled at 75 proof? I find the flavored versions outstanding in aroma but not quite as impressive in taste, perhaps because the base spirit is not of top-notch quality. The unflavored version, however, is very good.

TASTING NOTES

1822 ORANGE

Very light but honest and clean orange aroma. On the palate slightly oily in texture with the sweet flavor of oranges. As with the Citron, however, there is an underlying bitterness that also rather spoils the short finish. Makes a good mixer.

1822 ROSE

Powerful, very intense scent of rose petals. On the palate, very smooth and with an unbelievably concentrated and quite sweet flavor of roses. Just a touch of bitter spirit in the background. Long, very persistent finish. This is a remarkable feat of flavoring, so I have rated the brand highly, but I find it too perfumed, too sweet and overpowering, to drink by itself and can think of nothing to mix it with!

1822 COLA

This has the authentic, sweetish smell of diet cola with just touches of alcohol. Bitter on the palate, although the cola flavor does stand up well to begin with before getting rather swamped by some quite aggressive alcohol burn. Leaves a rather bitter aftertaste in the mouth. I have not rated this highly but some other people who have tasted it have been very impressed. Ignore the suggestion on the label to mix it with tonic and drink it chilled and neat.

Have a good look at the bottles as well. The larger, multicolored back label is designed to be looked at through the vodka, and produces a three-dimensional kaleidoscope effect.

Eldurís

SPIRIT FACTS

Owner Catco

Rectification plant Reykjavik, Iceland

Production 50,000 cases

Strengths both versions at 80 proof

Launched in 1988, this is another brand that was first developed for the booming U.S. market for Nordic vodkas. Despite encouraging initial sales, it had to be withdrawn from the market when its U.S. agent pulled out of its contract. But it has continued to do well in Iceland and is available in other Nordic countries and parts of Canada.

The brand is produced by Catco, the Clean Air Trading Company, which is the largest producer of vodka in Iceland, and also produces Tindavodka, the Icelandic schnapps Brennivín, and Lord Dillon gin. Its bottling plant in Reykjavik is one of the oldest in Iceland and has been in production since 1935, when prohibition was lifted.

RATING

Eldurís
★★

Eldurís Citrus
★★

The company does not distill itself, but buys in the finished vodka from outside suppliers. The spirit is triple distilled and made from high-quality Icelandic grain. Its main attribute, however, is that it is reduced to the desired strength with the addition of Icelandic water, which is renowned for its purity and clarity. Only natural essences of lemon and other citrus fruits are used in the production of the Citrus version.

These are two-well made, very clean vodkas with stylish packaging to match.

TASTING NOTES

ELDURÍS

Very, very neutral in aroma with just hints of ethyl alcohol. Thickish in texture with good smoothness and slight hints of quinine but very dry. A bit of fire on the finish. Drink this ice-chilled and neat.

ELDURÍS CITRUS

Upfront, concentrated and honest lemon aroma. Very clean and crisp on the palate with a strong lemony taste and just a bit of bitterness, but this disappears on the finish, leaving just a light and fragrant citrus flavor. Good enough to drink by itself and very good when mixed with tonic.

ELDURÍS
ICELANDIC
CITRUS
VODKA

750ml 40% alc./vol. 80° Proof

Finlandia

Spirit Facts

Producer Alko

Distillery Koskenkorva, Finland

Production 1.7 million cases

Strengths Finlandia 75, 80, 100 proof
Arctic Cranberry 80 proof
Arctic Pineapple 80 proof

First launched in 1970, Finlandia is regarded as Finland's finest and is produced by Alko, the state-owned distilling monopoly that also has the Koskenkorva brand. It has sales worldwide of about 1.7 million cases and has been the fastest-growing leading spirits brand in the world in recent years. A new U.S. distribution deal in 1996 should ensure wider availability to American consumers.

The vodka was until recently produced in the historic Rajamäki distillery some 28 miles from Helsinki, which first came into production in 1888 and has played such an important role in the development of vodka in Finland. Today, however, production has been moved to the Koskenkorva distillery in the northwest of Finland, which is closer to the country's grain belt. Only high-grade Finnish grain, mostly wheat, is used in the vodka's production.

Rating

Finlandia
★★★

Arctic Cranberry
★★★★

Arctic Pineapple
★★★

The equipment used for distillation is state-of-the-art and the computerized technology has been exported as far afield as Taiwan and India, and even to Scotland. Alko uses continuous stills, a double column for distillation and a triple column for rectification, which gets rid of the remaining fusel oils and methanol. It is then diluted to the required strength and the result is an excellent example of a very pure and clean "Western"-style, Nordic vodka.

TASTING NOTES

FINLANDIA

Crystal-clear with a clean, pure bouquet in the best Western style, but pungent and quite spirity even when bottled at 75 proof. Smooth on the palate but with a definite dry, almost salty bite. Excellent, clean aftertaste.
Mixes well but is also good enough to drink straight, preferably from the freezer.

ARCTIC CRANBERRY

Brilliant dark pink in color with mauve and orange tinges. Lovely bouquet of real cranberries with slight medicinal undertones. On the palate, very fruity and quite sweet but with no trace of the slightly bitter tang of fresh cranberry juice. Surprisingly waxy in texture with an outstanding balance of fruitiness, acidity, and alcohol. It gives a long lingering flavor in the mouth.
I am not persuaded by the producer's suggestion that it can be mixed with other fruit juices such as orange and grapefruit as I find that the flavors clash or smother each other. But it does make a wonderfully original and very refreshing long drink when mixed with tonic and ice. As this is undoubtedly one of the best and most honest-flavored vodkas on the market why not drink it straight and chilled? Alternatively, it is a lovely sipping vodka for after dinner.

ARCTIC PINEAPPLE

Light gold in color. Very pungent and intense, with the powerful scent of canned pineapple, which is strong enough to disguise the alcohol. Sweetish on the palate but prevented from becoming too cloying by the cut of the alcohol. Just a touch of sourness to the aftertaste but a good, persistent flavor. Drink it straight and chilled as the strong taste will kill the flavors of anything it is mixed with.

Having resisted the temptation to jump on the flavored-vodkas band-wagon for many years, Alko introduced the Arctic Cranberry version in 1994 and the Arctic Pineapple in the following year.

The exact recipe and production process are closely guarded secrets. But the company uses natural flavorings, essences, and pure fruit juices from which it has extracted undesirable elements such as pectins and acids that would impart "off" smells and flavors and make the vodkas cloudy. Both versions have outstanding color and an honesty of smell and taste that sets them well apart from most of their rivals.

This is one of the best ranges of vodka available.

Finlandia is one of the best ranges of vodka available. Flavorings used are all natural, and their outstanding color sets them apart from other flavored vodkas.

Fleischmann's

SPIRIT FACTS

Owner Barton Distillers

Rectification plants Owensboro, Kentucky; Los Angeles, California; Albany, Georgia

Production figures not available

Strength 80 proof

Founded in 1870, the Fleischmann Distilling Company made its name distilling gin, whisky, and brandy. When vodka became popular in the United States it added one to its portfolio and the company eventually became part of Glenmore Distilleries, itself bought by the British spirits company United Distilleries in 1990. Today it is part of the huge conglomerate, Barton Brands, the fourth-largest distilled spirits marketer in the United States, and the second-largest vodka and tequila supplier. Barton acquired United Distillers Glenmore brands in 1995.

RATING
Fleischmann's Royal
★

The company buys in neutral grain spirit from outside sources and then rectifies and filters it in its plants in Kentucky, California, and Georgia. The result is a typically American vodka, very neutral in taste, without much character, but made honestly enough and good as a mixer.

TASTING NOTES

FLEISCHMANN'S ROYAL

Almost odorless with just hints of sweetness. A little thick in texture and smooth but with some burn developing toward the end. Sweetish in taste and finish. A reasonable, very neutral mainstream vodka to be used as a mixer.

French Alps

SPIRIT FACTS

Owner Cognac Landy
Production figures not available
Strength 80 proof

This elegantly packaged French vodka is produced by the small, independent firm of Landy, near the town of Cognac and is well known for its luxurious Cognac presentations for the duty-free industry.

The vodka is made from a special strain of wheat which produces very pure starch and is grown in the fertile Brie region of France. Distillation takes place only during the winter and is done in small

RATING

French Alps
not graded

batches in pot stills, and the water used for dilution is drawn from wells fed from the Alps. The vodka is filtered three times, first through charcoal and then through a calcium filter that has been electrostatically charged to attract congeners. After three months in stainless-steel tanks for harmonization, the spirit is given a final filtration through a fine, natural-cotton filter just before bottling. All told, the company claims that its production process takes three times longer than that of most vodkas because of the batch distilling and the slow filtration process.

TASTING NOTES

FRENCH ALPS

Not entirely clean on the nose, slightly sweet with slight touches of DMTs. Better on the palate, sweetish with an underlying bitterness. Quite thick in texture with a slight burn. Leaves a bitter aftertaste. Definitely a mixer.

Fris

SPIRIT FACTS

Owner Danisco Distillers
Distillery Aalborg, Denmark
Production figures not available
Strength 80 proof

The bottle is the epitome of Scandinavian style and elegance and the good news is that the quality of the contents matches that of the packaging.

"Fris" means frost and ice in Danish, and this vodka was especially developed by Danisco Distillers, Denmark's leading spirits distiller, to be served straight from the freezer. The water used is softened by the removal of its hard minerals, which are replaced by sodium ions. This makes it thicker so that it does not freeze. Only the whole grain is used for the wash and the spirit is distilled through a six-column apparatus. The initial filtration is through two 264-gallon, active carbon columns. The vodka is then "polished" through two membrane filters to remove any carbon dust.

Produced in Danisco's historic Aalborg distillery in Northern Jutland, this is an interesting, high-quality vodka to look out for and drink when almost frozen.

RATING

Fris
★★★

TASTING NOTES

FRÏS

Pours thickly into the glass when heavily chilled. Very neutral in aroma. Very, very smooth on the palate with a thick, almost oily texture with a light, subtle spiritiness. Very dry on the finish.

Glenmore

SPIRIT FACTS

Owner Barton Brands

Rectification plants Owensboro, Kentucky;
Albany, Georgia

Production figures not available

Strength 80 proof

This is another vodka brand that was owned in the early 1990s by the British multinational United Distillers, part of the Guinness company, which bought it in 1991 and forged it into United Distillers Glenmore. As the double-headed eagle on the label suggests, it is now part of Barton Brands, which bought it in 1995 with a number of others, such as Schenley and Mr Boston, when United Distillers decided to concentrate on its Bourbon brands and imported Scotches and gins.

The brand is rectified in Barton's Kentucky and Georgia production facilities and is made entirely from high-class grain.

I find this brand rather disappointing and would use it only as a mixer.

RATING

Glenmore Special
Reserve

★

TASTING NOTES

GLENMORE SPECIAL RESERVE

Very neutral in bouquet. Thickish in texture but with quite aggressive alcohol burn. Slightly sweet with hints of caramelization. Medium-length finish in which the strong alcohol burn totally takes over. Many will find the rating to be rather generous. Use as a mixer.

Gorbatschow

SPIRIT FACTS

Owner Henkell & Söhnlein Sektkellereien
Distillery Berlin, Germany
Production 1.4 million cases
Strengths Blue label 75, 80 proof
Black label 100 proof.
Red label 120 proof

The mid-1980s handed this brand a marketing opportunity that other spirits producers can only dream of. Gorbatschow was firmly established as West Germany's leading vodka brand but few people had ever heard of it outside the country. Then came glaznost and the sensational rise of President Gorbachev. Marketed as the "Vodka of Friendship," the brand was launched internationally in 1987 and its sales just went through the roof, surpassing the one-million-case mark by the beginning of the 1990s. Today this momentum has eased slightly but it is still a huge brand with sales in over 50 countries and with a strong franchise in Eastern Europe. The white dove of peace is still carried proudly on its label.

The origins of the brand go back to pre-revolutionary Russia, when the Gorbatschow family were vodka distillers in St Petersburg and, like so many others, are said to have been suppliers to the Czar. With other eminent distillers such as the Smirnovs and the Aslanovs, the Gorbatschows fled Russia after the Bolshevik Revolution and settled in Germany. By 1921 they had started to distil again in Berlin, catering mostly for

RATING

Gorbatschow
★★

the Russian émigrés. In the post-war period, Gorbatschow's sales spread to other parts of Germany and it now holds 45 percent of the German market. The brand is owned by the wine producer Henkell & Söhnlein.

Gorbatschow is made entirely from wheat and is distilled and rectified in the same distillery in Berlin. Continuous stills are used and the vodka is then filtered twice through charcoal.

This is a difficult brand to judge, because I find a great difference in the quality of the different strengths. My advice is to go for the 100 proof version, use it as a mixer, and just use less than you would normally.

As a sideshow, the company produces a feisty, crisp pre-mix Gorbatschow & Lemon in a can. Tasting of bitter lemon, it has a strength of 10 proof, but you can always add a bit more vodka to give some extra bite.

TASTING NOTES

GORBATSCHOW

The 80 proof version has unpleasant cabbagey odors, indicating that some DMTs have got through the distillation and rectification process. Very sweet on the palate, with cabbagey flavors and touches of burned sugars. Smooth to begin with but with growing alcohol burn.
The 100 and 120 proof versions, however, are very different, clean and pure on the nose with just traces of alcohol.
Still rich in style on the palate but showing none of the impurities of the lighter version.
A bit of burn.
These are very much better vodkas and the rating is for them and not the 80 proof version.

Gordon's

SPIRIT FACTS

Owner United Distillers

Rectification plant Plainfield, USA

Production 2 million cases

Strengths 80, 100 proof
Orange and Wildberry 60 proof
Citrus 70 proof

As is the case with its stablemate Tanqueray Sterling, this is a famous name better known for gin than vodka. The difference is that, while all Tanqueray vodka is distilled in the United Kingdom, Gordon's vodka is made primarily in Plainfield, Illinois and in Canada for the local market. Like Sterling, however, It is only really available in the U.S., which is the only market for the flavored variants.

Gordon's vodka was first produced in Illinois during the 1950s when vodka's popularity was in the ascendency in the United States, and it is now a major brand. All of it is rectified in plants owned by United Distillers, applying all the expertise built up by the company during over 200 years of gin distilling. Only high-grade

RATING

Gordon's Vodka
★★★

Gordon's Citrus
★

Gordon's Wildberry
★

Gordon's Orange
★★

grain from the Midwest is used and rectification is carried out in continuous stills. Filtration is through charcoal.

For the flavored variants only natural fruit essences, such as orange from the West Indies, are used, and these are added after distillation. All three of them are clear in color.

All the vodkas tasted were produced in the United States. Use all four versions as mixers. The three flavored versions make interesting vodka tonics.

TASTING NOTES

GORDON'S
Very, very neutral on the nose with just a faint hint of ethyl alcohol and no evidence of any impurities. Very rich on the palate but not at all cloying because of the dryness of the alcohol, which gives excellent balance. Very smooth— wonderfully so with hardly a trace of needle—a good mellowness, and big mouth feel. Particularly recommended if you like a richer, fuller style. Use in cocktails.

GORDON'S CITRUS
Oil from orange skins imported from the West Indies is added as an enhancer to the essence of lime and lemon in this vodka, and their delicate and honest aromas mingle pleasantly. Smooth on the palate but with a touch of sourness and slightly sweet. The fruit flavors fade quickly on the finish.

GORDON'S ORANGE
Very light on the nose and one-dimensional. The orange flavor is more pronounced than in the Citrus and it is quite sweet and tangy. It also lingers longer in the mouth.

GORDON'S WILDBERRY
Very powerful aroma, much stronger than in the other two flavored versions. Sweet, slightly flowery and cloying on the palate, with a strong, spirity background taste. Not for me.

Huzzar

SPIRIT FACTS

Owner Irish Distillers
Distillery Cork, Ireland
Production 100,000 cases
Strength 75 proof

The Irish know a thing or two about distillation and there is even evidence that it was Irish monks who kept the art alive during the Dark Ages. Today this proud tradition is maintained by the Irish Distillers company, a subsidiary of the French giant Pernod Ricard, which produces the Jameson and Bushmills brands, considered by many to be the finest whiskeys in the world. In white spirits it produces Huzzar and the famous Cork Dry Gin.

Huzzar is made of a wash of maize with a little malted barley thrown in. It is then triple distilled, as most Irish spirits are, at the historic Midleton distillery in County Cork and percolated through active carbon beds for filtration. The result is a very Western vodka to be used as a mixer.

RATING

Huzzar
★

The Midleton distillery, which houses the largest copper pot still in the world, is open to the public and has a visitors' center. It is well worth visiting. But do not expect to be told about vodka; whisky is their pride and joy.

TASTING NOTES

HUZZAR

Very clean in bouquet with just light traces of alcohol. This is reflected on the palate, where it is light, very smooth, but slightly, just slightly, caramelized. Short and neutral on the finish.

Ikonova

SPIRIT FACTS

Owner Boisset
Distillery Nuits St Georges, France
Production figures not available
Strength 75 proof

This is another vodka from the stable of the Boisset group, based in the Burgundian village of Nuits St Georges, which also produces the 1822 range of flavored vodkas through its J. Morin subsidiary.

There is frustratingly little information about this brand, which is available only in France. The base is 100 percent

RATING

Ikonova
★★

grain and either the raw spirit or the finished vodka is imported from abroad—but from where appears to be a closely guarded secret, as is the production and filtration process. I find this secrecy difficult to understand but the end product is not at all bad. The packaging is also impressive, although not as innovative as that of the 1822 range.

TASTING NOTES

IKONOVA

Extremely neutral in aroma, and I find this one of the most neutral vodkas featured in this book. Thickish and slightly oily on the palate, very smooth and with just a touch of background needle. Clean in taste and with a reasonable finish.

There is not much else to say. This is a very Western vodka, although not as light and crisp in texture as the others. Use as a mixer.

Iskra

SPIRIT FACTS

Owner Fourcroy
Distillery Brussels, Belgium
Production 3,000 cases
Strength 75 proof

*I*skra, the *Spark,* the title of the Bolshevik newspaper founded by Lenin. This, however, is a Belgian brand, despite its Russian name and the double-headed imperial eagle on the label, and is produced by the family-owned company of Fourcroy, which first entered the spirits business in 1892 with the Mandarine Napoleon liqueur. The company also produces the Van Hoo vodka brand.

RATING

Iskra
★★

Iskra was first launched in 1978 and is sold mostly in the Benelux countries. It is made entirely from molasses, which gives it a sweetish taste, and is produced in the company's distillery in Brussels in continuous stills. Filtration is through activated carbon.

The result is a good, middle-of-the road vodka very much in the Western style.

TASTING NOTES

ISKRA VODKA

Neutral and odorless on the nose. Very clean, sweetish in style as one would expect from a molasses vodka, but not cloying. Quite gentle and smooth on the palate. Nice long, slightly sweet finish.

This is a good example of a well-distilled molasses vodka. Quite nice on its own well chilled, but better as a mixer.

Monopol

SPIRIT FACTS

Owner A.S. Remedia
Distillery Kiiu, Estonia
Production figures not available
Strength 75 proof

Like all other countries of Eastern Europe, Estonia has a long tradition of distilling vodka and, in Viru Valge, it has a brand with sales of over a million cases. This brand is not as big but it is still an important one in the region and gives a good idea of the Estonian style.

RATING

Monopol
★★

Monopol is made by the Remedia company in the town of Kiiu. Local, high-grade grain, an important factor in the quality of Estonian vodka, is used, and the vodka is then distilled according to a recipe that the company claims goes back to the fifteenth century. Not much more information is available, although I suspect that a little bit of sugar is added to soften the taste. This is accepted practice in Estonian distilling. It explains the vodka's rich character, more in the Russian than the Western style.

TASTING NOTES

MONOPOL

Very pungent, sweetish nose with strong hints of amyl alcohol. Slightly oily and thick in texture, very smooth with just a bit of alcohol needle coming in toward the end. Sweet and rich in style but avoids being cloying because of the needle. Medium length, sweetish finish with touches of caramel. I find it better at room temperature than chilled. Not a mixer.

Mr Boston

SPIRIT FACTS

Owner Barton Brands

Rectification plants Owensboro, Kentucky;
Albany, Georgia

Production figures not available

Strength 80 proof for both lines

There is very little to say about this rather cheaply packaged US vodka, which is part of a family that includes an egg nog and a blackberry-flavored brandy.

As part of United Distillers Glenmore, it was sold to Barton Brands in 1995 and is still rectified and filtered in Kentucky and Georgia.

TASTING NOTES

MR BOSTON

Clean on the nose, slightly spirity and sweet. On the palate, sweetish but clean. Harsh with some astringency and with quite aggressive alcohol burn. Quite persistent on the mouth and the alcohol burn swiftly disappears. Some will find my rating overgenerous. Use it as a base for a long drink, not for a cocktail.

MR BOSTON'S RIVA

Slightly cabbagey in aroma with medicinal notes of amyl alcohol. Sweet on the palate with quite a bit of burn in the mouth. Short on the finish.

This is a battling brand but does not taste as bad as it looks, and its quality is relatively good considering its price. Strip away the harshness and you are left with a reasonably correct Western vodka. The same cannot be said about Riva, the brand's second string.

RATING
Mr Boston
★
Mr Boston's Riva
not graded

Puschkin

SPIRIT FACTS

Owner Berentzen
Distillery Haselünne, Germany
Production 500,000 cases
Strengths Puschkin Vodka 75 proof
Puschkin Red 35 proof
Puschkin Black Sun 33.2 proof

I was initially put off by the coloring of the flavored, apéritif versions of this brand but tasting them was a revelation. The clear vodka is a well-made, carefully distilled spirit and, unlike other producers, Berentzen obviously uses this rather than a cheaper base spirit in the preparation of the flavored versions. These are very exotic in flavor and taste remarkably honest, so can be a great party trick.

Originally the vodka was produced by the well-established German company of König & Schlichte in Berlin. It was, however, taken over in 1990 by the larger Berentzen company, one of Germany's largest schnapps producers, founded in 1758 and still family-owned. Since then the vodka

has been improved and repackaged, and is now the second-largest-selling vodka in Germany.

Berentzen buys its spirit from the Bundesmonopolverwaltung, the German state spirits-producing monopoly. The spirit is made from grain, potatoes, and molasses, which explains its rich character. It is double distilled in continuous stills and is then rectified and filtered in

RATING

Puschkin Vodka
★★

Puschkin Red
★★★

Puschkin Black Sun
★★★

Berentzen's small but highly efficient plant in the pretty town of Haselünne in northwest Germany. For the flavored versions the vodka is blended with juices: concentrated blood-orange juice for the Puschkin Red, and that of wild berries and the root *eleutherokokkus* from the steppes of Siberia for the Black Sun.

Puschkin Red received a gold medal at the Wine and Spirits Competition in London in 1995 and was elected the most successful spirits innovation in Germany in the same year.

The Haselünne plant is open to the public and has a museum showing the history of distillation, well worth visiting.

TASTING NOTES

PUSCHKIN VODKA

Very light, clean, and neutral bouquet with very slight medicinal undertones. In the mouth, very sweet but showing no signs of caramelization. Spirity but smooth with a quick finish. This is a well-distilled vodka that will appeal to those who like a rich, sweet style.

PUSCHKIN RED

Cloudy and orangey-pink in color. Very pleasant and honest aroma of blood orange. Sweet but sharp and not at all cloying on the palate with an intense flavor. Good length in the mouth.

PUSCHKIN BLACK SUN

Black with violet tinges. The aroma and taste of this vodka are primarily those of grapefruit, but the taste of berries also comes through. Sweet but not cloying. Drink by itself well chilled.

Rasputin

SPIRIT FACTS

Owner Dethleffsen

Rectification plant Flensburg, Germany

Production 1,000,000 cases

Strengths Rasputin Magic 80 proof
Rasputin Prestige 80 proof
Rasputin Citron 80 proof
Rasputin Cranberry 80 proof

He looks at you sinisterly not just once but four times altogether. Twice from the label on the bottle, once from the neck collar, and a fourth time from a small collarette, which shines in different colours when tickled. It is Grigory Rasputin, the mad, debauched monk who played such an important role in the destruction of the Romanov dynasty.

The brand is produced by Dethleffsen, a German company that can trace its origins back to 1738, when it was founded by Christian Dethleffsen in the Baltic port of Flensburg. Initially it was a trading company dealing in, among other things, brandy and rum and within a century it had built its own distillery. In 1870 the company was split into two by Hermann Georg and Diederich Dethleffsen with one branch focusing on the lumber business and the other on the

RATING

Rasputin Magic
not graded

Rasputin Prestige
not graded

Rasputin Citrus
★

Rasputin Cranberry
★

distillation of spirits. Today the spirits company is still owned by the descendants of the founder and produces a wide range of spirits, including aquavits and rums.

Rasputin Magic was launched in the late 1980s and soon carved out a market for itself, particularly in Eastern European markets. The higher-quality Prestige line completed the range in 1995.

Despite its long tradition of distilling white spirits, Dethleffsen buys in raw grain spirit which it rectifies, dilutes, and filters at its plant in Flensburg. The formula for the flavored versions is a closely guarded secret.

I find this a disappointing range of vodkas. But other drinkers obviously disagree; the brand sells over a million cases a year, in countries as diverse as Australia, Mongolia, and Israel.

TASTING NOTES

RASPUTIN MAGIC

Very neutral in aroma to begin with but then a distinct smell of caramel emerges. Quite harsh on the palate where the heavy taste of burned sugars becomes obvious.

RASPUTIN PRESTIGE

Slightly sweet in aroma with citrus touches. This one is smoother than the Magic but again the cloying taste of toffee and burned sugars is apparent.

RASPUTIN CITRON

Very pungent but a bit chemical in aroma. Smooth enough and quite sweet and long-lasting but, again, rather chemical in taste. Acceptable as a mixer.

RASPUTIN CRANBERRY

Dark pink in color with orange and violet tinges. Quite intense on the nose with pleasant cranberry aroma and slight medicinal undertones. Sweetish on the palate, slightly medicinal and with a bit of alcohol burn. Nice, long-lasting aftertaste. In my opinion the best in the range.

Royalty

SPIRIT FACTS

Owner Hooghoudt Distillers B.V.
Distillery Groningen, Netherlands
Production figures not available
Strength 80 proof

This vodka was first produced by Hero Jan Hooghoudt in 1888 and on its 100th anniversary Hooghoudt Distillers were appointed purveyors to the royal court. It is made entirely from wheat harvested in Northern Holland and water purified by forcing it through special filters under high pressure. It is distilled at comparatively low temperatures using a special vacuum technique to avoid caramelization, and then rectified through a four-column system. Filtration is done upward through five columns of active carbon made from peat.

RATING
Royalty
★★★

The result is a very, very good vodka, undoubtedly one of the best in the Western style.

TASTING NOTES

ROYALTY

Very light on the nose with just touches of very clean and delicate aroma of ethanol in the background. No hint of impurities. On the palate very smooth and silky, quite sweet and rich with good mouth feel. The alcohol needle becomes apparent only after it has lingered on the palate. Good persistence in the mouth.

Schenley

SPIRIT FACTS

Owner Barton Brands
Rectification plants Owensboro, Kentucky; Albany, Georgia; Los Angeles, California
Production figures not available
Strength 80 proof

This is an elegantly packaged U.S. vodka first produced by the well-known distillers and spirits importers Schenley Distillers. For many years the company was the force behind the Dewar's White Label Scotch brand in the United States before being bought in 1987 by the brand's owner, the British multinational United Distillers, which is part of Guinness plc. In 1995 the brand, along with several others and production plants in Kentucky and Georgia, was purchased by Barton Brands.

There is not much information available on the brand but it is still produced in Kentucky and Georgia where it is distilled from grain.

Definitely a mixer.

RATING

Schenley Superior
not graded

TASTING NOTES

SCHENLEY SUPERIOR

To begin with, very neutral and clean on the nose, but then develops a strong odor of toffee and burned sugars. Very sweet in style and with strong, cloying toffee taste and a little needle. Spirity finish with a bit of fire. Disappointing.

Selekt

SPIRIT FACTS

Owner Richmond Distillers
Distillery Warrington, UK
Production figures not available
Strength 80 proof

This is another brand from the Luxembourg-based Richmond Distillers, so forget the Russian imperial eagle and the Cyrillic script on the label—this vodka is as Western as they come. The company is partly owned by G. & J. Greenall, which has been distilling white spirits in England since 1761 and is also the owner of the Black Death brand.

RATING
Selekt
★★★

The company buys in raw spirit in the United Kingdom and then rectifies it in Greenall's highly efficient and functional plant in Warrington, Cheshire. Filtration is through carbon filters. As is the case with Black Death the company will not reveal what raw material is used but my guess would be molasses rather than grain because of its rich style.

In my opinion this is by far the better of the company's two brands.

TASTING NOTES

SELEKT

Very clean on the nose with, perhaps, just traces of quinine in the background. The quinine is a bit more pronounced on the palate and adds to the quite rich style of the vodka. It is, however, crisp and light in texture and very clean. Quite a long finish.

I find this a very pleasant vodka that I do not mind drinking on its own.

Skol

SPIRIT FACTS

Owner Barton Brands

Rectification plants Owensboro, Kentucky; Albany, Georgia; Los Angeles, California

Production figures not available

Strength 80 proof

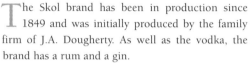

The Skol brand has been in production since 1849 and was initially produced by the family firm of J.A. Dougherty. As well as the vodka, the brand has a rum and a gin.

The brand was briefly under British ownership in the early 1990s, when United Distillers bought it as part of Glenmore; but it was sold to Barton Brands along with others in 1995.

The vodka is rectified in Barton's production plants in California, Kentucky, and Georgia, and is made from grain.

RATING

Skol Premium

★

TASTING NOTES

SKOL PREMIUM

Totally odorless without even touches of alcohol. Sweetish on the palate with a bit—a very little bit—of grain flavor. Acceptably smooth, although a bit of needle does develop. Sweet, rather short finish.

This has a bit more character than most U.S. vodkas, but I still recommend it as a mixer.

Smirnoff

SPIRIT FACTS

Owner The Pierre Smirnoff Company

Distillery produced in numerous distilleries around the world

Production 14.4 million cases

Strengths Smirnoff Red 75, 80 proof
Smirnoff Blue 100 proof
Smirnoff Citrus 75 proof

In the West, Smirnoff is now almost synonymous with vodka, and it is one of the greatest success stories of the spirits industry of the post-war era. Worldwide sales are now not far off 15 million cases a year and its producer, the Pierre Smirnoff Company, a subsidiary of the British multinational International Distillers & Vintners, proudly claims that about 500,000 bottles are drunk around the world every day.

It was in 1818 that Ivan Smirnov, as the family name was then spelled, first registered the company of I.A. Smirnov & Family in

Moscow, 1902. With the launch of Smirnoff Black, the vodka has returned to its roots.

Moscow and started distilling vodka in some buildings that had been damaged during the Napoleonic War. But it was his great-nephew, Piotr Arsenyetvitch, who gave the company its first great impetus. Burning with ambition, he bought out his cousin's shareholding in the business and re-built the distillery. He

RATING
Smirnoff Red and Blue Labels
★★
Smirnoff Citrus
★

also established the company's headquarters in the Pyatnitskaya building in central Moscow, which is now Russia's leading forensic institute and where the remains of Czar Nicholas II and his family were finally validated.

His big breakthrough came in 1886 at the Nizhni Novgorod Exhibition. Piotr had a bear in a cage on his stand and this attracted the attention of Czar Alexander III. Having sampled his vodka he immediately appointed the Smirnovs as sole purveyors of vodka to the Imperial Court. Similar appointments to the Courts of Sweden and Spain soon followed, and exports to Western Europe and even the U.S. began.

By the turn of the century the company was producing 3.5 million cases of vodka a year and employed 1,500 people. Revenue had reached 38 million rubles, some $20 million, making the Smirnovs one of the richest families in the world.

All this was blown away by the Russian Revolution when the Bolsheviks confiscated all private industries in Moscow, including the Smirnov distillery, which was turned into a state garage. Nicolai Smirnov was to die penniless in Moscow many years later but his brother Vladimir managed to escape after facing a firing squad several times and being reprieved at the last moment.

In exile, Vladimir tried to reconstruct the family business but with little success. After failures in both Constantinople and Poland he ended up with a small distillery in Courbevoie outside Paris. It was here that he met Rudolph Kunett, one of his former grain suppliers, and sold him the exclusive rights and license to all the company's alcoholic beverages in the

Smirnoff's unique distillation process—each drop of spirit passes through seven tons of charcoal resulting in a vodka of immense purity.

United States, its territories, Canada, and Mexico. In 1933 the Ste. Pierre Smirnoff Fils, as the family name was by then spelled, was incorporated in New York and the rest of the story on how the brand was to revolutionize spirits-drinking in the United States is told in another chapter.

Today Smirnoff is produced in several different countries, including Russia and Poland. But the Pierre Smirnoff Company claims that, as it is always produced following the exact formula that was used by the Smirnovs in Moscow, the spirit has a quality and character that is always exactly the same. I am not quite persuaded by this theory, but there is little doubt that the brand is remarkably consistent.

TASTING NOTES

SMIRNOFF RED and BLUE

The 75 proof version is absolutely clean and odorless on the nose. Smooth and light on the palate with just a bit of needle, very clean and pure with just a little residual sweetness. Slightly spirity on the finish. The 80 proof, however, does have traces of cereal and alcohol on the nose and is a little richer on the palate, but still bears the brand's hallmarks of purity, smoothness, and lightness. So does the equally rich Blue Label, although, as one would expect, it does have some alcohol burn when drunk neat. It is, however, a lot less aggressive than that of many other brands bottled at 80 proof.

For me, Smirnoff sets the standard against which all other Western vodkas should be measured. Some are undoubtedly better. But an awful lot more are worse. Considering the volume that the company produces this is a very great achievement.

SMIRNOFF CITRUS

Very light on the nose, but clean and with an honest lemony aroma. Quite sweet on the palate and a bit one-dimensional in taste with a bit of alcohol burn. Good persistence of flavor on the finish.

Smirnoff is always made from high-quality neutral grain spirit, which is then rectified in the company's own plants in high-column plate stills, a process that takes 24 hours. It is then blended with water that has been filtered through active carbon and passed through deionization columns. At a strength of 114 proof, the spirit is then pumped upward through a series of up to 10 columns containing activated charcoal made from the hardwood family of trees such as maple, birch, and beech. Each drop of spirit passes through seven tons of charcoal and it takes a minimum of eight hours for the filtration process to be complete. Finally the spirit is reduced to the desired strength with the addition of more demineralized and purified water.

The result is a spirit of immense purity. Whether or not it bears any similarity to the vodka that was produced by the Smirnovs in Moscow, however, is another matter. The company has recently launched Smirnoff Black, which is produced exclusively in Russia through a totally different process (see p. 165). For these tasting notes I used a 75 proof version of the Red Label produced in the United Kingdom, an 80 proof Red Label and a Blue Label produced in the United States.

Piotr Arsenovich (Pierre Smirnoff) established the company's headquarters in the Piatnitskaya building in central Moscow.

Tanqueray Sterling

SPIRIT FACTS

Owner United Distillers
Distillery Laindon, England
Production 250,000 cases
Strengths 80, 100 proof

Tanqueray is a name more associated with gin than vodka, and Tanqueray Gin, the biggest imported gin brand in the United States, is considered by many to be the best in the world. Sterling Vodka, however, is a spirit more than worthy of carrying such an illustrious name.

RATING

Tanqueray Sterling
★★★★

Tanqueray Sterling
Citrus
★★★★

The Tanquerays were a French Huguenot family exiled to England in the early eighteenth century, and David, the founder of the English side of the family, became the Official Silversmith to the royal court. It was his descendant Charles who first started distilling gin at a location believed to have been in Bow in the

East End of London in 1830. Later, he transferred his operation to the north of the city and, in 1898, the company was merged with the larger, more famous Gordon's. The two brands, however, have maintained their separate identity to this day. Now part of United Distillers both the gin and the vodka are produced in a state-of-the-art distilling facility in Laindon in Essex, to which some of the original distilling equipment was transferred in 1989, the year Sterling was launched.

Tanqueray Sterling's master distiller, Hugh Williams, who has worked for the company for most of his life, uses especially selected spirits made mostly from wheat, which have been double-distilled in slow, continuous stills. Then comes a third distillation that sets Sterling apart from most of its competitors, this time in a copper pot still known as Old Tom, which was built in 1780. The spirit is then charcoal-filtered to ensure that it achieves an unsurpassed level of purity. Citrus, the lemon and lime flavored variant, has natural essences of both fruit added after distillation.

TASTING NOTES

TANQUERAY STERLING

This is a very superior vodka, packaged in a frosted bottle that exudes British understated elegance. Crystal-clear and absolutely clean on the nose without any hint of impurities. Slightly sweet and mellow and soft on the palate with outstanding smoothness coming from its third distillation. There is little trace of spiritiness until the finish. As clean and pure as you can probably get. Undoubtedly one of the great Western vodkas.

Sip it neat straight from the freezer. Alternatively add a small dash of dry vermouth for a really memorable dry vodka Martini.

The result is two outstanding vodkas that can look any other great vodka squarely in the eye. Unfortunately for non-Americans, their distribution is mostly limited to the United States.

Tanqueray Sterling's master distiller, Hugh Williams.

TASTING NOTES

TANQUERAY STERLING CITRUS

Very subtle, delicate and complex on the nose with wonderful hints of lemon and lime. Not as overpowering as many citrus-flavored vodkas. Very dry, crisp and smooth on the palate with a fascinating combination of lemon and lime flavors that are not cloying in any way. It is much more complex and less one-dimensional than most of its rivals with a good persistence of flavor.

Again this can be sipped neat when ice-chilled. Alternatively it makes a good vodka tonic with no need for a slice of lemon or lime.

Tindavodka

SPIRIT FACTS

Owner Catco
Rectification plant Reykjavik, Iceland
Production 10,000 cases
Strengths 75, 80 proof

Launched in the early 1970s, this brand is available only in Iceland, where it has been remarkably successful, being one of the three best-selling vodkas on the market from day one.

Tindavodka is produced by the Icelandic company Catco, which also produces the much superior Eldurís brand. The finished vodka is bought in and bottled in the company's plant in Reykjavik, and is made from grain which is then triple distilled. Icelandic water, said to be the clearest and purest in the world, is used to dilute it to the required strength. The vodka is bottled at both 75 and 80 proof and the tasting notes are for the latter version.

RATING

Tindavodka
—not graded

TASTING NOTES

TINDAVODKA

Very, very neutral on the nose and almost odorless. Very sweet and a bit cloying on the palate, tasting strongly of toffee with a bit of bite but acceptably smooth. The toffee flavor is strong again on the finish.

Van Hoo

SPIRIT FACTS

Owner Fourcroy
Distillery Eeklo, Belgium
Production figures not available
Strength 80 proof

This is probably the youngest vodka brand in the world, having been launched in the fall of 1996. But it is produced in Belgium's oldest distillery in Eeklo, in a region famous for its distilling traditions.

The Van Hoorebeke family were originally brewers but turned to distilling jenever gin in the middle of the eighteenth century. The original distillery was destroyed just after the battle of Waterloo in 1815, but another one soon took its place and today Van Hourebeke is Belgium's oldest jenever brand owned by Fourcroy, best known for its Mandarine Napoleon liqueur, but also the distiller of the Iskra brand of vodka.

RATING

Van Hoo
★

Van Hoo vodka is made entirely from grain and is distilled in both continuous and pot stills. Filtration is through charcoal. The distillery accepts visitors and has a museum.

TASTING NOTES

VAN HOO

Distinct notes of citrus and quinine on the nose. On the palate the quinine is even more pronounced, giving the vodka a mouth-filling richness. Quite aggressive needle, and the vodka does lack smoothness, which is surprising, since pot stills are used. Good persistence in the mouth. Would score more highly if it were smoother.

Von Haupold

SPIRIT FACTS

Owner Rives Pitman S.A.
Distillery Puerto de Santa Maria, Spain
Production 50,000 cases
Strength 75 proof

Von Haupold is distilled in the small sherry and brandy town of Puerto de Santa Maria in southern Spain and is owned by the giant Osborne, one of Spain's largest brandy distillers, and the Haupold family, direct descendants of

RATING
Von Haupold
★★

the founder. Rives Pitman was founded in 1880 by Augusto Haupold, who came from Germany and was one of the first to distill gin in Spain. They are one of the largest gin distillers in the country.

The vodka is distilled and rectified in the company's own plants, enabling it to have control over the entire process. Only the best alcohol, triple distilled in columns more than 65 feet high, is used for the vodka, which is then bottled at 75 proof.

TASTING NOTES

VON HAUPOLD
Pungent on the nose, but pleasantly so with delicacy and a strong hint of citrus. Some lemon essences have undoubtedly been added. Because of its triple distillation, very smooth on the palate, with a rich, mouth-filling taste and consistency. Long, persistent flavor.

Vikingfjord

SPIRIT FACTS

Owner Arcus Produkter
Distilleries 4 distilleries in Norway
Production 25,000 cases
Strengths 80, 100 proof

This unusual potato vodka from Scandinavia was originally developed in 1985 to cash in on the phenomenal popularity of Nordic vodkas in the United States. It was first made by a joint venture between the Norwegian spirit production monopoly Vinmonopolet and the U.S. distiller Heublein of Smirnoff fame. However, when Heublein was taken over by the British multinational International Distillers & Vintners (IDV), soon after the launch they were told to withdraw from the project because IDV already distributed two Nordic vodkas—Finlandia and Absolut—in the United States. The brand was then subsequently sold to Arcus Produkter, a Norwegian company.

Arcus buys the raw spirit from four potato distilleries in Norway, where most of it is distilled by continuous distillation with small quantities of pot still spirit added to enhance the aroma. The company then rectifies it using its own plant in Oslo,

TASTING NOTES

VIKINGFJORD

The aroma of this vodka is so neutral that it is virtually nonexistent. Rather sweet and heavy on the palate, very smooth and mouth-filling. Clean but short and slightly spirity aftertaste.
Try it ice-chilled.

increasing the strength from 190 to 192 proof. It is then diluted to the required strength using water extracted from glaciers, which is submitted to ion-exchange treatment to remove the calcium. Filtration is in three stages using sand and carbon filters.

RATING
Vikingfjord
★★

Most distillers dismiss potatoes as an inferior raw material because it is difficult to break down the starch and convert it into sugar. I tend to agree with them, but this is an exception and is a well-made and clean vodka, proving that potato-based vodkas can be of good quality. Unfortunately it is only available in Scandinavia and the United States.

Try this unusual potato vodka ice-chilled.

Virgin

SPIRIT FACTS

Owner Virgin Spirits
Distillery Girvan, Scotland
Production 208,000 cases
Strengths 75, 80, 100 proof

This is the product of two famous companies in the United Kingdom: William Grant & Sons, the family-owned Scotch distiller of Glenfiddich and Grant's Standfast fame (which has been in the business since 1887), and Virgin Enterprises, one of the companies owned by the high-profile entrepreneur Richard Branson, better known for his airline and ballooning exploits.

As with most products under the Virgin brand, this is a stylishly packaged vodka and it has achieved a number of firsts. It was the first vodka to be advertised on TV in the United Kingdom, the first to feature a gay kiss in its TV advertising and the first brand to sponsor a weekend's programming on television.

The brand was first launched in London in 1994 and nationally in the United Kingdom in the following year, and it has been remarkably successful ever since. It is now the third-largest mainstream vodka brand in the United Kingdom and is widely available in Western Europe and North America, and duty-free, where it is in a distinctive blue, frosted bottle.

RATING

Virgin Vodka
★★

Virgin is produced from grain and distilled at the Girvan distillery in Ayrshire in the Scottish Lowlands. This is one of the largest suppliers of grain spirit in the country and provides the base spirit for the Grant's blended whiskys. The master distiller uses an eight-column apparatus that puts the spirit through three complete distillation processes. Such is the purity of the emerging spirit that no great filtration process is needed.

This is a very modern, very trendy vodka, but it is difficult to say very much about it, since it is a characterless, neutral spirit, exactly what the producers want it to be. Definitely a mixer—and stick to the lower- strength versions.

TASTING NOTES

VIRGIN VODKA

Very, very neutral on the nose with just hints of alcohol if you dig deep enough. Slightly thick in texture, quite sweet but very clean. Very smooth with hardly a trace of needle. Short on the finish. The 100 proof version is even more neutral on the nose than the 75 proof, but the sample I tasted did have some traces of caramelization.

Vladivar

SPIRIT FACTS

Owner Whyte & Mackay Group
Distillery Glasgow, Scotland
Production figures not available
Strengths Vladivar 75 proof
Vladivar Gold 114 proof

Few people who were in the United Kingdom in the 1970s and early 1980s will have forgotten the famous "Ze vodka from Varrington" adverts for this vodka when it was owned by G. & J. Greenall, based in Warrington, Cheshire. The brand has moved on since then, however, is now a bit less high-profile, and is owned by the Glasgow-based Whyte & Mackay Group, itself a subsidiary of the mighty American Brands, which produces Jim Beam Bourbon and the Kamchatka and Wolfschmidt vodka brands in the United States.

RATING

Vladivar
★★

Vladivar is made from molasses and distilled in one of Whyte & Mackay's distilleries in Scotland. The spirit is triple distilled in a continuous still then filtered through charcoal beds for extra purity.

TASTING NOTES

VLADIVAR

Exceptionally neutral and clean in aroma. Very light and slightly sweet in the mouth, very smooth with just touches of needle. Clean and quite short finish. That is it! There is nothing more to say. This is the epitome of a good British vodka, distilled to the highest level of purity possible. So if this is what you want then you need go no farther.

POLAND

It is estimated that there are about one thousand brands of Polish vodka on the market today. However, most of them are available only in certain parts of Poland. The following directory section, therefore, cannot pretend to be a comprehensive examination of the entire Polish vodka industry.

We have, however, included all the major brands that have some distribution outside Poland and those new, deluxe brands that are being exported. This gives a good idea of the quality and variety that the Polish vodka industry is capable of.

Poland, however, does have some problems. The old Communist system of vodka production and export has been swept away and has been replaced with one that has not quite been perfected yet. Its basis is the 25 Polmoses, production plants that buy in raw alcohol from agricultural distilleries and rectify, filter, dilute, and bottle it as vodka. All these

Krakow, Cloth Hall, Town Square. The basis of Polish vodka production consists of 25 Polmoses – production plants that own all major brands jointly.

Polmoses also own the major trademarks such as Wyborowa, Żytnia, and Zubrowka jointly so can produce vodka bearing those names.

The problem is that some Polmoses have better production facilities than others, and take more care in the production process than others. They use different water for dilution and grain from different parts of the country. The quality of these brands, therefore, does tend to vary slightly.

Luckily, Agros Trading, the old state-owned trading group, has won the rights to Wyborowa and Zubrowka on most foreign markets. As it uses only the leading Polmoses in Zielona Góra and Poznan as suppliers, the consistency and quality of these brands on foreign markets are pretty even. Their quality in some parts of Poland itself and in countries where Agros still does not own the trademark, however, can vary.

In general, therefore, the Polish system is working better than the Russian one, ensuring that Polish vodka is more consistent in quality and style than Russian vodka. The Polish authorities are also working hard to iron out the remaining difficulties.

Good Polish vodka has its own very particular style and the brands featured in this book are a good reflection of this. Enjoy them!

Belvédère

SPIRIT FACTS

Owner Polmos Zyrardów
Rectification plant Zyrardów, Poland
Production figures not available
Strength 80 proof

This was the second deluxe vodka to be launched in Poland after Chopin and copied many of its packaging innovations, such as the satiny finish to the bottle and the window on the front through which the illustration on the back can be seen magnified by the vodka. It has, however, been very successful in getting distribution outside Poland.

The vodka is produced in Zyrardów, a town just to the southwest of Warsaw, by the local Polmos, which buys in raw alcohol from agricultural distilleries and rectifies it in its own plant. It is then multifiltered and reduced to 80 proof using water from the Polmos's own wells. I find the packaging of this vodka to be superb, but its quality to be very disappointing for a deluxe brand. The illustration on the bottle depicts the official residence of the Polish president in Warsaw.

RATING

Belvédère
not graded

TASTING NOTES

BELVEDERE

Strong whiff of toffee on the nose. Sweet and cloying on the palate with strong caramelization. Some alcohol burn. Powerful finish in which the toffee flavor predominates. This is an indifferently distilled vodka.

Bols

SPIRIT FACTS

Owner Unicom-Bols Group

Distillery Oborniki, Poland

Production the joint venture produces 1.6 million cases of the Bols and Pani Twardowska brands a year

Strength 80 proof

This vodka is the product of a joint venture between the Dutch alcohol producer Bols Royal Distilleries and the private Polish distiller Unicom, formed in 1995. The brand was launched in Poland in the same year alongside its sister brand Pani Twardowska and has grown to become the fastest-growing vodka brand in Poland, It is also exported to Western Europe.

The Dutch company was founded in 1575 when Lucas Bols first started distilling white spirits in a shed outside Amsterdam and flavoring them with the spices and fruits brought to the Netherlands by Dutch merchantmen from around the globe. Today it is one of the most famous liqueur and jenever gin producers in the world and has injected centuries of distilling experience into the joint venture. Unicom first started distilling in 1993 at Oborniki on a site chosen for its deep wells, which yield water of great purity. The joint venture also distills the Russian Stolichnaya and Moskovskaya brands under license.

Bols vodka is made from high-quality rye spirit, which the company rectifies to a high

RATING

Bols Vodka

★★

degree and then dilutes with demineralized and distilled water from its own wells. It is then filtered three times through carbon filters, allowed to rest for a day, and then bottled.

The result is an interesting vodka. Its producers have obviously applied Western standards of distillation and rectification to get a spirit of great purity and consistency, but have tried to produce a vodka with a Polish soul in which the flavor of the traditional rye prevails. It is, however, less traditional in style than Pani Twardowska.

Drink it neat and slightly chilled.

TASTING NOTES

BOLS VODKA

The Western influence is evident in the aroma of this vodka, which is very neutral, with just a little alcohol and hardly any trace of rye. On the palate, however, the spirit's Polish origins start to come out: rich, very clean, and pleasant rye flavor. Not quite as smooth as it could be, with a perceptible alcohol burn. Nice length to the finish, but would score more highly if it was just that little bit smoother.

Chopin

SPIRIT FACTS

Owner Polmos Siedlce
Distillery Siedlce, Poland
Production figures not available
Strength 80 proof

L aunched in the autumn of 1993, this excellent vodka soon made a significant impact on the Polish vodka industry. It was the first of the deluxe vodkas made by a single Polmos to the very highest quality and presented in luxurious and very innovative packaging. Despite retailing in Poland for about double the price of standard vodkas, it soon met with enough success to persuade other Polmoses to launch their own versions and there are about 15 of them on the market today.

Chopin is produced by the Podlaska Wytwórnia Wódek Polmos in the eastern city of Siedlce, founded in 1896, and the whole concept was developed by its management. They were the first to think of a tall, thin bottle for greater shelf stand-out and the satiny finish to the glass to preserve the vodka inside. They were also the first to think of the window on the front of the bottle and to put Delacroix's portrait of the famous composer on the rear so that it is magnified by the vodka. Once the blueprint had been developed it was then put into practice by a French company, which manufactured the first bottles.

Siedlce, however, is as proud of the vodka as it is of the packaging and it claims to have two important advantages over its rivals.

First, it draws all its raw materials, which in the case of Chopin are rye and potatoes, from the so-called "ecological" part of Poland in the eastern half of the

RATING

Chopin
★★★★

Fryderyk Chopin,
Poland's favorite son.

country, which remains relatively free of pollution. And secondly it is the only Polmos in the country that has invested in its own distillation facilities. So while its rivals have to buy their raw spirit from agricultural distillers, Siedlce has full control over the production process. It has also invested in an advanced water processing plant supplied by the US manufacturer Culligan to ensure that the water it uses, from its own well, is highly purified. The result is a very special product that has stirred some controversy in Poland. In 1996, the composer's sister's great-granddaughter protested against the use of her ancestor's name for commercial purposes. The result was that the Ministry of Culture submitted a motion to the public prosecutor's office in Siedlce to ban the use of the name and the image of Chopin by the Polmos, arguing that putting the name of the great Fryderyk on a bottle of spirit offended the memory of Poland's favorite son. It was only the intervention of the Ministry of Commerce that saved the vodka from being withdrawn.

The vodka in European markets is made from rye. But a version for the U.S. market made from the Strobava strain of potatoes is being developed. Tasting notes here are for the rye variety.

It is an excellent vodka, and I suggest you ignore the collar booklet's recommendation to drink it in "one swift shot" or mixed with fruit juices. Chill, and then sip it neat to appreciate its quality.

TASTING NOTES

CHOPIN

Beautifully soft and delicate rye nose. Good intensity of flavor in the mouth, smooth and well balanced with the sweetness of the rye counterbalanced by a slight, background alcohol burn which is by no means unpleasant. Middle-length aftertaste. This is an excellent Polish vodka, expertly distilled, the type that first persuaded me that the Poles can make the best vodkas in the world.

Cracovia

SPIRIT FACTS

Owner Polmos Kraków
Rectification plant Krakow, Poland
Production figures not available
Strengths Supreme 84 proof. Classic 80 proof

This is the second of Polmos Kraków's deluxe vodkas launched in 1996, just a couple of years after the Polmos entered the market with Fiddler. It is a very different vodka, however, more traditional, as its elegant but conservative packaging suggests, and with no apple spirit added. The crest on the bottle is the coat of arms of the city of Krakow.

RATING

Cracovia
★★★

The Polmos, a few minutes' drive from historic salt mines that have been worked for over six centuries, buys in high-quality raw spirit from agricultural distilleries and rectifies and filters it in its own plant. The grain used is mostly rye, which explains its rich and slightly sweet character, and the water that is used for dilution is from the Polmos's own well.

Cracovia is bottled at two strengths, the Supreme at 84 and the Classic at 80 proof.

TASTING NOTES

CRACOVIA SUPREME

Very clean but very light nose with background hints of rye that are difficult to detect. Full and sweet on the palate, oily in texture with a bit of fire from the extra alcohol. Very light hints of caramelization. Nice, rich finish.

This is a big, interesting vodka that will appeal to those who like a richer, sweeter style. Drink it neat and chilled as its strong character does not lend itself to mixing.

Fiddler

SPIRIT FACTS

Owner Polmos Kraków

Rectification plant Krakow, Poland

Production figures not available

Strength 78 proof

I enjoyed the very humorous, tongue-in-cheek packaging of this brand. The cap is covered with a little plastic bowler hat and the neck collarette plays the tune of "If I Were a Rich

RATING

Fiddler

★★★

Man" from *Fiddler on the Roof* when opened. But make no mistake about it, this is a serious vodka, the first of Polmos Kraków's deluxe brands and one that can compete in quality with any other deluxe brand in Poland.

This is a highly rectified rye spirit, diluted to the right strength with water from the distillery's own well. What sets it apart is that a little vanilla is added to enhance and enrich its aroma and flavor, and the result is a very modern vodka. Serve it neat and well chilled.

TASTING NOTES

FIDDLER

Very clean and almost odorless on the nose. Lightly sweet with the rye flavor beautifully rounded off by the taste of vanilla. Very smooth and mellow with no alcohol burn. Excellent, full finish. A very, very well-made vodka with no rough edges, distinctly Polish but with just that subtle point of difference.

Jarzębiak

SPIRIT FACTS

Owner the trademark is owned by several
Polmoses in Poland

Rectification plant several in Poland

Production figures not available

Strength 80 proof

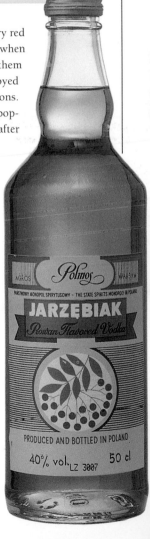

In Poland they say that, if rowanberries are very red in the fall, a hard winter will follow. Quite when someone first thought of flavoring a vodka with them will never be known but Jarzębiak has been enjoyed in Poland for generations. It is the second-most popular flavored vodka after Zubrowka.

RATING

Jarzębiak
★★★★

Rowanberries, together with dried tropical fruits, are infused in high-quality vodka and small amounts of sugar and grape distillate are added. The spirit is then aged for a short period in oak barrels to give it a little color. The tasting notes are of a sample from Polmos Zielona Góra.

TASTING NOTES

JARZĘBIAK

Very pale gold in color with hints of green. Acrid is how its aroma is often described, but I find it to have a complex, very intense berry fruitiness on the nose. Very dry in taste but with a great intensity of fruit flavors and a light background fire from the alcohol. Wonderful, dry finish with the taste of fragrant berries, which lingers for a long time in the mouth. This is unique and deserves the highest rating. Enjoy it either lightly chilled or at room temperature.

Królewska

SPIRIT FACTS

Owner Polmos Zielona Góra
Rectification plant Zielona Góra, Poland
Production figures not available
Strengths 80, 84 proof

This is the deluxe vodka from the famous Lubuska Wytwórnia Wódek Gatunkowych distillery in the southern city of Zielona Góra and is the work of its head distiller and quality controller Elzbieta Goldymka, one of Poland's new breed of distillers.

Królewska means royal in Polish and the stained-glass window on the bottle is taken from the medieval church of St Mary's in Krakow, once the capital of Poland and the residence of its kings. The crowned eagle is the royal coat of arms and the three turrets that of the city of Krakow.

Launched in 1995, the spirit is made from premium rye and, being a luxury vodka, is heavily rectified and filtered at the Zielona Góra plant. The tasting notes are for the 84 proof version.

RATING

Królewska
★★★

TASTING NOTES

KRÓLEWSKA

In my opinion this has the most pleasing nose of any Polish vodka, delicate, soft, and pure, with a lovely rye aroma. To begin with, sweetish and delicate on the palate, a little oily and silky without being cloying but it then develops some needle because of the extra strength, which I find a little aggressive. Hints of caramelization also begin to appear. Good rye finish. This is a characterful, very good vodka, which misses being outstanding by a whisker because of the slightly burned taste. Chilling it down subdues the caramel but the burn, which some drinkers will enjoy, is still evident.

Krupnik

SPIRIT FACTS

Owner the trademark is owned by several
Polmoses in Poland

Rectification plant several in Poland

Production figures not available

Strength 80 proof

The early civilizations of Eastern Europe made
mead from wild honey and, once distillation
had been discovered, the combination of vodka
and honey would have
been a natural step. The
recipe for this brand, or
a close approxim-
ation, is said to date back to as early as the
eighteenth century.

RATING
Krupnik
★★★★

Krupnik is made of rectified spirit in
which bee honey and several spices are
steeped. It would also appear from its
aroma and taste that it is given some aging
in the barrel The tasting notes are for a
sample made at Polmos Zielona Góra.

TASTING NOTES

KRUPNIK

Almost mahogany-brown in color with some
copper tinges. Complex on the nose with the
aromas of honey, cinnamon, and cloves
predominating. Slightly spirity. Sweet but not
at all cloying on the palate, very intense and
concentrated, complex with the flavors of the
different ingredients marrying beautifully.
Honey, cinnamon, ginger, cloves, and a touch
of woodiness. Very smooth with just the right
amount of spirit. Wonderfully complex finish
with good persistence.

Luksusowa

SPIRIT FACTS

Owner the trademark is owned by several Polmoses in Poland

Rectification plant several in Poland

Production 1.7 million cases

Strengths 80, 90, 100 proof

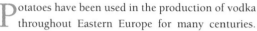

Potatoes have been used in the production of vodka throughout Eastern Europe for many centuries. Luksusowa, however, is one of the only brands that appears to be proud of still maintaining this long tradition with, in this case, the words "Made from Select Potatoes" displayed on its label.

RATING

Luksusowa
Luxury Vodka
★★★

Luksusowa is made from special strains of potato that have been especially adapted for vodka production. It is difficult to extract all the impurities created during the fermentation of the wash, so the spirit is distilled four times. This is an interesting vodka that will appeal to those who like the heavier style.

TASTING NOTES

LUKSUSOWA

Pungent, sweetish nose with medicinal tones. Very oily, initially a little sweet but developing a dry, rather austere style. Smooth and with just a pleasant touch of fire. Nice long finish with a bit of sweetness.

This is a characterful potato vodka that contrasts interestingly with the lighter, more delicate, traditional Polish rye vodkas. Drink it straight as its power blends uneasily with mixers such as tonic and orange juice.

Pani Twardowska

SPIRIT FACTS

Owner Unicom-Bols Group
Distillery Oborniki, Poland
Production figures not available
Strength 80 proof

There is a legend behind the illustrations of a woman and a moon traveler on the label of this vodka. Pani means Mrs. in Polish and Mrs. Twardowska's husband was a magician in sixteenth-century Krakow who made a Faustian pact with the devil, signed in his own blood. In return for supernatural powers during his lifetime, Twardowski agreed to surrender his soul to the devil if ever he went to Rome. For years he thoroughly enjoyed life and his special powers until one day the devil caught him drinking in a tavern called Rome. Twardowski, however, reminded him of a clause in the pact saying that, to claim his soul, the devil had to fulfill three conditions. The first was to make a whip out of sand, which he had no problem in doing. The

second was that he should have a bath in holy water, which he did rather reluctantly. The third condition, however, was that he should live with Mrs. Twardowska for one year and, when he was reminded of it, the devil flew away and was chased to the moon by Twardowski riding on a rooster. So there he is, sitting on the moon and toasting the health of his wife, whose bad temper saved his soul from eternal damnation.

Quite why someone should wish to call a vodka after this legend I do not know, but it is an unusual vodka in that it is one of the only ones in Poland produced not by a state Polmos but by the privately owned distillery Unicom, which started distilling in 1993 and subsequently signed a joint venture deal with the Dutch drinks company Bols two years later. Both the Bols and the Pani Twardowska brands were launched in 1995.

The distillery uses demineralized and distilled water from its own well to dilute high-quality rye spirit to the required strength. It is then carbon-filtered three times to ensure a consistently high level of purity.

At time of writing the brand is available only in Poland, but the Unicom-Bols Group has plans to start exporting it extensively.

RATING
Pani Twardowska
★★★

TASTING NOTES

PANI TWARDOWSKA

Lightweight but very pleasant rye aroma, very clean. Rich, slightly medicinal rye flavor on the palate, very smooth, slightly oily and with just a bit of alcohol burn. Good, long-lasting finish.

This is a very well-distilled, traditional Polish vodka that is very different from the Bols brand that is distilled in the same plant.

Pieprzówka

SPIRIT FACTS

Owner the trademark is owned by several Polmoses in Poland

Rectification plant several in Poland

Production figures not available

Strength 90 proof

The origins of this vodka are buried in history. All we know is that the flavoring of vodka with pepper is as long a tradition in Poland as it is in Russia and it is a style that is still popular in the country today. There are in fact several other pepper brands that are made in Poland by the individual Polmoses, but Pieprzówka is the main one.

RATING

Pieprzówka

★

The brand is said to be made from highly rectified spirit, which is then infused with red and black pepper pods, which give it its color, and with a bit of paprika.

TASTING NOTES

PIEPRZOWKA

Light red with bluish tinges, almost violet in color. On the nose some touches of DMTs from the base spirit come through, which rather spoil the pleasant aromas of spices and pepper. Initially sweetish on the palate with distinct flavors of paprika and pepper. Very smooth and hot on the palate but less aggressively so than in other pepper vodkas. On the finish, the flavors tend to fade rather quickly, leaving only a pleasant glow on the tongue. This would rate more highly if it were made with better-quality base spirit. An interesting vodka all the same.

Premium

SPIRIT FACTS

Owner Polmos Poznan
Rectification plant Poznan, Poland
Production 2.4 million cases
Strength 80 proof

Founded in 1823 by a Prussian cavalry regiment during Poland's long and unhappy occupation, Polmos Poznan or the Poznánskie Zaklady Przemyslu Spirytusowego Polmos to give it its full name, stands next to the Malta lake in the suburbs of Poznan. Its rectification plant, a huge, charmless industrial operation, is just a few miles away on the outskirts of the city.

Poznan has been the most important center of vodka production in Poland for centuries and the Polmos has maintained this tradition. It is the largest and one of the most advanced production centers in the country, supplying about 20 percent of the vodka consumed in Poland and much of the vodka exported under famous brand names such as Wyborowa, Luksusowa, and Żytnia. In common with most of the leading Polmoses, however, it also now produces its own brand, Premium, which it launched in 1993 and is now the third-largest-selling

RATING

Premium
★★

Premium Special
★★

Premium Citron
★

Premium Peach
★★★

Polish vodka brand. The Premium Special is one of the new generation of Polish deluxe vodkas.

The Polmos buys in raw spirit with a strength of 184 proof from agricultural distillers, which it then rectifies in a two-column Barbeta apparatus. The first column, with 38 trays, removes the impurities that boil at lower temperatures, such as methanol; and the second, with 70 trays, extracts the heavier substances, such as fusel oil. The spirit emerges from the process with a strength of 193 proof and is then reduced to the required strength using demineralized water from the Polmos's own wells. Filtration is through charcoal and carbon plate filters.

By law, only natural ingredients can be used to flavor vodka in Poland and Polmos Poznan uses some 15 different natural essences for its flavored versions.

The clear vodkas in this range are undoubtedly excellently made. But I do not find them particularly Polish in character and I miss the rye aroma and flavor that I regard as the hallmark of a great Polish vodka.

TASTING NOTES

PREMIUM VODKA

Very neutral on the nose with just very light background notes of rye. Very rich and sweet in flavor with definite traces of burned sugars but very smooth, with hardly any needle. Good persistence of flavor in the mouth.

PREMIUM SPECIAL

Light in aroma and very neutral, even more neutral than its clear colleague. Very sweet and a bit cloying on the palate with light traces of caramelization but a bit of cereal flavor does come through. Again, very smooth with good, lingering flavor. I find both these vodkas a little sweet, a characteristic that remains even when you serve them ice-chilled.

PREMIUM CITRON

The aroma of lemon is light, delicate, and pleasant but it does not disguise that of the base cereal spirit. I find it a bit disappointing in taste as the citrus flavor is too light, allowing the cereal flavor to all but dominate. In texture a bit heavy and oily and lacking in crispness. Good finish in which the two distinct flavors manage to marry. Honestly made with an obviously natural flavoring.

PREMIUM PEACH

This is much better, with a clean, fragrant aroma of peaches almost jumping out of the glass. Slightly bitter in taste, but this counterbalances the natural sweetness of the fruit, which could otherwise be cloying. Just a touch of burn and good length with the taste of peaches staying in the mouth. Try this neat and chilled. Otherwise it makes an exotic vodka tonic.

Starka

SPIRIT FACTS

Owner the trademark is owned by
several Polmoses in Poland

Rectification plant several in Poland

Production figures not available

Strength 100 proof

I t is very difficult to classify this as a vodka, since it
is a cereal-based spirit that is aged in the barrel. It
is, therefore, far more akin to a whisky in some ways
than a normal clear and highly purified vodka and,
when I first tasted it at Polmos Poznan, its woody,
slightly sweet aroma put me immediately in
mind of Bourbon.

Nevertheless, this is a highly revered
brand in Poland, and when it was served to
me it was poured lovingly by the distillery's
deputy director, not into the traditional
Polish stemmed shot glass but into a small
brandy balloon.

The origins of the brand are said to go
back to the sixteenth century and the
tradition is that, in the houses of the gentry,
vodka was poured into an old wine barrel at
the birth of a baby girl to mature until her
wedding. Unfortunately this practice has now
probably all but disappeared, although
modern producers have at least maintained
part of this tradition.

Starka is the only Polish vodka made from
unrectified but high-quality rye spirit that is
aged in barrel for a minimum of ten years. As
it is made in several Polmoses, different types

RATING

Starka

★★★★

of barrels are used. The most usual, however, are those used for the maturing of the sweet Hungarian Tokay, which give it its first touches of sweetness of aroma and taste. Some of the sweet, raisiny Malaga fortified wine from southern Spain is also added to the spirit before bottling. The result, of course, is a very different vodka, one of the few made in Poland in which the producers have attached more importance to aroma and flavor than to purity.

This is undoubtedly a post-dinner, fireside spirit, particularly as it is usually bottled at 100 proof. I suggest that you do not chill it the way some people do, but drink it the way it was served to me in Poznan: at room temperature and in a glass that helps you to really capture its complex aromas and flavor.

There is also a rarer Russian version of this vodka, which is made and aged in a similar way, but is infused with the leaves of apple and pear trees to give it an extra fruity dimension.

The tasting notes here are of a sample that was made at the Zielona Góra distillery.

Starka is aged in barrels in the same way as whisky.

TASTING NOTES

STARKA

Dark gold in color with very light green tinges. Intense, complex aroma reminiscent of a good-quality marc with scents of vanilla and chocolate. Concentrated, spirity, dry with just touches of winey sweetness, and very woody on the palate with flavors of vanilla and chocolate.

Some alcohol burn, as can be expected from a high-strength spirit. Persistent, very pleasant aftertaste. I am not persuaded by this vodka, finding it a bit too woody and, at times, quite mouth-puckering because of its long aging and high strength. But there is no doubt that this is a very interesting spirit, full of complexity and quite unlike any other I have ever tasted.

Wísniówka

SPIRIT FACTS

Owner the trademark is owned by several
Polmoses in Poland
Rectification plant several in Poland
Production figures not available
Strength 80 proof

The flavoring of spirits with cherries is popular in Poland, and this is its favorite cherry vodka.

In contrast with other spirits in this style produced in Poland, this has no other ingredients, such as almonds, added, making it a highly rectified spirit in which natural cherries have been steeped. I would describe it as a sweet rather than semisweet

RATING
Wísniówka
★★

vodka, as it is often described. In Poland it is often drunk as an accompaniment to coffee or dessert. The brand is produced in several Polmoses and the tasting notes are from a sample from Zielona Góra.

TASTING NOTES

WISNIOWKA
Lovely, deep cherry-red. Intense scent of cherries on the nose with just touches of pepperiness. Very rich and sweet, very concentrated fruitiness of flavor with enough alcohol bite to balance the sweetness and make it warming. Just a bit of bitterness of flavor does emerge toward the end. Long-lasting, sweet, and fruity finish.
I find this a very pleasantly flavored vodka but not as interesting or complex as some of the other Polish classics. Very much an after-dinner spirit.

Wyborowa

SPIRIT FACTS

Owner the trademark is owned by several
Polmoses in Poland

Rectification plant several in Poland

Production estimates vary

Strength Wyborowa 76, 80,
90, 100 proof
All flavored versions at 80 proof

Industry estimates on the worldwide sales of this brand vary from 18.1 million cases a year to 4.39 million, which is quite a discrepancy. What matters, however, is that it is now generally acknowledged to be the largest-selling Polish brand in the world and is increasingly easy to find in the West.

Wyborowa was first launched in Poland in the 1920s but was not exported until some 50 years later. During the 1960s it established quite a reputation for itself in Europe, particularly in the United Kingdom, where it became the largest-imported vodka brand. Then it just faded away and it is only recently that its fortunes outside Poland have started to revive.

Today it is made in the majority of the country's Polmoses but most of what is

RATING

Wyborowa
★★★★

Wyborowa Lemon
★

Wyborowa Orange
★

Wyborowa Peach
★★

Wyborowa Pineapple
not graded

exported is from either the Zielona Góra or Poznan rectifying plants, which guarantees its consistency. The vodka claims to be the only one the world produced exclusively from rye and from the hardier, winter strains that are planted in the fall and harvested the following summer. These are grown in the northwestern part of Poland, where the milder climate and the light soils combine to yield a healthy cereal crop. Importantly, the rye grown in the region is high in starch, which is then easier to break down into sugar and ferment into alcohol.

Distillation is carried out in agricultural distilleries and the raw alcohol is then highly rectified in Zielona Góra and Poznan. Triple

TASTING NOTES

WYBOROWA

Light, fragrant, slightly sweet rye nose with just a touch of spirit. Very pleasantly sweet on the palate with just enough needle to give it a bit of bite with a wonderful background taste of rye. Nice length to the finish with a good persistence of grain flavor. If you like the Polish style of vodka this is as good an example as you will get. And it will come at half the price of the new breed of deluxe Polish vodkas. Drink it neat and slightly chilled.

WYBOROWA LEMON

Very light in aroma but the scent does appear honest. On the palate, lacks intensity of flavor, but sweet in style, and I think I can detect some flavors of melon alongside those of lemon. Very smooth with only touches of needle and a lightweight but pleasant finish. Drink straight.

filtration, through charcoal and carbon plate filters, then follows and the vodka is diluted to the right strength with water from the plants' own wells, which has been softened and demineralized.

I do have a soft spot for the clear version, and think its quality justifies its growing worldwide success. I am not, however, as fond of the flavored versions. By law only natural ingredients can be used in Poland and I find their flavoring to be very honest. But they are very light in flavor, and I think disappointingly so.

The tasting notes are from samples from Zielona Góra, all at 80 proof. Apart from the flavors tasted, the brand also has a pepper-flavored version, which is more difficult to find.

TASTING NOTES

WYBOROWA ORANGE

Rather disappointing in aroma with only a very light scent of oranges, although it is honest enough when you can find it. Light, too light in my opinion, in flavor. Slight alcohol burn and a bit thick and oily in texture. Better on the finish with good persistence of taste but with some bitterness and burn.

WYBOROWA PEACH

Wonderful scent of real peaches. Light in peach flavor and dry with a bit of background alcohol burn. Quite oily and heavy in texture. Good length to the finish with just a touch of bitterness.

This will appeal to those who like dry, flavored vodkas but it lacks the lightness of texture of the better Western brands.

WYBOROWA PINEAPPLE

Good, natural aroma of sweetish, canned pineapple chunks but very light. Thickish in texture, rather bitter with the pineapple flavor very much in the background. Aggressive alcohol burn in the mouth, which also overpowers the weak and rather thin flavor of the finish.

Zubrowka

SPIRIT FACTS

Owner the trademark is owned by several Polmoses in Poland

Rectification plant several in Poland

Production figures not available

Strength 80 proof

For me the unique taste and aroma of Zubrowka will always be associated with my first visit to Warsaw and I will never forget the waiter's look of approval when I ordered one as an apéritif before dinner in a restaurant in the old quarter.

This is a vodka that you either love or hate, and I am always fascinated by people's reaction when they first taste it. Somerset Maugham loved it. "It smells of freshly mown hay and spring flowers, of thyme and lavender, and it is so soft on the palate and so comfortable, it is like listening to music by moonlight," he wrote in *The Razor's Edge*.

Zubrowka is flavored with bison grass or *Hierochloe odorata* and *Hierochloe australis*, which grows in small clumps in the glades of the Bialowieza forest on the border between Poland and Russia. This is the habitat of the rare European bison, which was nearly made extinct during World War Two but is now once again thriving in the wild.

The grass is harvested by hand in early summer when its aromatic qualities are at their best and it has not yet been yellowed

RATING

Zubrowka Bison Vodka
★★★★

by the sun. It is then dried, cut to the right size, and bound in bunches before delivery to the distillery. There it is spread out over sieves and vodka is forced through it several times until an aromatic essence is obtained. This is then mixed with high-quality, dry-rye vodka following a traditional— and very secret—formula, is allowed to stabilize for several days for the aromas and flavors to harmonize, is filtered and bottled. The final touch is that a blade of bison grass is put into every bottle by hand.

No one will ever know when this vodka was first made, but traditionally it was a hunter's drink served at the end of the day's shoot. Legend has it that it imparts the bison's strength to the drinker and it is also said to have medicinal properties. In Poland it has overtaken Jarzębiak to become the country's most popular flavored vodka, and it is becoming increasingly available on foreign markets.

A word of warning. Zubrowka is produced by several Polmoses and I have found it to vary a little in quality. There is no doubt, however, that this is a unique vodka, despite there being a Russian version called Zubrovka. I prefer to drink it neat and well chilled, but it is also the base for the Bitter Bison cocktail, in which it is mixed with sweet vermouth and lemon juice. Alternatively, mix one measure of it with three of apple juice and serve well chilled.

The tasting notes are from a sample produced at the Zielona Góra distillery in southern Poland.

TASTING NOTES

ZUBROWKA BISON VODKA

Very pale green in color with yellow tinges. I have always found that this has an initial bouquet of marzipan, which doesn't give way to Maugham's "freshly mown hay" until it's been some time in the glass. Immensely intense in flavor, complex with marzipan, fresh-cut grass, sweetish rye, and medicinal flavors. Smooth on the palate with a slight background burn of alcohol. The persistence of flavor is immense. Drink enough of it and the taste will be with you for days.

Because of its unique but very assertive character, this is an extremely difficult vodka to be objective about. As I have said, you will either love it or hate it.

Extra Żytnia

SPIRIT FACTS

Owner the trademark is owned by several
Polmoses in Poland
Rectification plant several in Poland
Production 2.7 million cases
Strength 80 proof

This is another vodka with a long history in Poland, and the word Żytnia is used to denote the smile on the face of a village elder or mayor, presumably after he has had a glass or two. Up until recently it was Poland's favorite brand but it has now been overtaken by Wyborowa and

RATING

Extra Żytnia
★★

its sales have halved in recent years as Polish vodka consumption declines. It is still, however, the second-largest selling Polish vodka in the world.

The base spirit is made from high-quality rye and is then rectified in several Polmoses all around the country. Small quantities of well-matured apple spirit and some natural fruit flavorings are added to round it off. The sample tasted here is from Polmos Zielona Góra.

TASTING NOTES

EXTRA ŻYTNIA

The apple spirit is immediately discernible in the aroma and mingles pleasantly with that of the base rye spirit. Good rye flavor in the mouth, slightly spirity and heavy in texture with the apple spirit giving it a welcome extra dimension. Smooth and rounded with just a little needle. Good persistence of flavor with a pleasantly sweet finish.

Moscow, St Basil's. The Russian vodka industry has begun to attract foreign investment, but most Russian vodkas come to us courtesy of Sojuzplodoimport, the ex-state-owned trading group.

RUSSIA

Since the collapse of Communism in the Soviet Union the Russian vodka industry has begun to attract some foreign investment. Pernod Ricard from France has formed a joint venture with the Sokolovo distillery in Siberia to produce Altaï. Dethleffsen of Germany has joined up with the Livis distillery in St Petersburg to produce Ultraa. And the Pierre Smirnoff Company is now producing Smirnoff Black at the Cristall distillery in Moscow.

These new ventures have added an interesting new dimension to Russian vodka. But most of the Russian vodkas available in foreign countries still come to us courtesy of Sojuzplodoimport, the ex-state-owned trading group.

Sojuzplodoimport is no longer state-owned but now belongs to a group of ten leading distilleries—the most important being in Moscow, Kaluga, St Petersburg, Samara, Irkutsk, Kaliningrad, and Kursk—which supply it with vodka.

The problem with the system is that each one of these distilleries can produce the vodka bottled under the different brands. So Moskovskaya Osobaya, supposedly Moscow Special, can just as well be made in Samara as in Moscow. Sibirskaya, supposedly Siberian vodka, can be made in Moscow or in St Petersburg. The different brand names, therefore, denote more of a style than anything else.

This has one great weakness. However much Sojuzplodoimport argues that it does not matter in which distillery the vodkas are made, since the distillation procedure is always the same, there is no doubt that there is a difference between, say, a Stolichnaya made in Moscow and one made in Kursk. The distillers are, after all, using different water and often different base cereals. The care taken in vodka production can also vary from distillery to distillery.

And this is at the root of Russian vodka's greatest weakness, its inconsistency. Stolichnaya can be a great vodka one day but not quite as good the next.

In the tasting notes in this section of the directory, therefore, I have tried to give no more than an idea of the general quality and style of the different brands. But judging Russian vodkas is very difficult, so take these, and the individual ratings, as a general guide only.

Altaï Siberian

SPIRIT FACTS

Owner Pernod Ricard Altaï
Distillery Sokolovo, Russia
Production 700,000 cases
Strength 80 proof

Produced under a cooperation agreement between the distillery and the French giant Pernod Ricard, Altaï is one, if not the only, vodka produced using Siberian raw materials only. It is made purely from wheat of a strong strain, grown on the Siberian Plain. The water used to dilute the spirit to the required strength is drawn from the rivers of the Altaï mountains. The vodka is triple distilled in continuous stills and is filtered through activated charcoal.

RATING

Altaï Siberian
★★

I approached this vodka with some misgivings, since the production process sounds very similar to that of the classic and better-known Sibirskaya. But the French influence has obviously made itself felt and the two vodkas are very different.

TASTING NOTES

ALTAI SIBERIAN

There is a strong element of amyl acetate on the aroma of this vodka, which is a great pity. Sweet, very rich and oily with good mouth feel. Very smooth but with a little background burn, suggesting that some glycerine has been added to smoothen it out. Good long, lingering flavor. This is a big, characterful vodka and I would have rated it higher had it been more correct in aroma. Drink it straight and chilled.

Krepkaya

SPIRIT FACTS

Owner V/O Sojuzplodoimport
Distillery several in Russia
Production 6 million cases
Strength 112 proof

The word means strong in Russian and this vodka is undoubtedly that, weighing in at a frightening 112 proof and making it one of the strongest spirits in the world. In a cold climate strong spirits have the advantage of not freezing as easily as those of lower alcoholic strength. They are also lighter and less bulky to transport, because they can be diluted to the required strength at their destination, an important factor in a vast country, particularly in the days of horse-drawn transport.

RATING

Krepkaya
★★★

This is a typically Russian vodka, made predominantly of wheat with some other cereals such as rye and oats added in small quantities. It is distilled in continuous stills and then filtered through charcoal and quartz for purity. The only real difference is that less water is added than to any other Russian vodka.

TASTING NOTES

KREPKAYA

Big, pungent aroma with some hints of acetone. Characterful, rich, and quite sweet on the palate with some good grain flavors, although these are all but masked by the alcohol burn. The addition of a little water subdues this and the vodka then becomes smooth, although the fire is always evident on the finish, which is long and fragrant. A very good, very Russian vodka.

Moskovskaya Osobaya

SPIRIT FACTS
Owner V/O Sojuzplodoimport
Distillery several in Russia
Production 9 million cases
Strengths all lines 80 proof

Along with Stolichnaya this is Russia's most famous vodka, but its sales have been taking a battering recently. In 1995 they are estimated by industry sources (the *SpiritScan* trade journal) to have been of just over 9 million cases, a fall of 45 percent in five years. Nevertheless it is still the world's third-largest vodka brand and the tenth-largest spirit brand.

Moskovskaya Osobaya means Moscow Special in Russian and the brand is also sometimes called the "Gold Medal" vodka because of the medals that are proudly displayed on its label. William Pokhlebkin claims that this is the only classic Russian vodka because it has all the "hallmarks of a true vodka," namely that it is 80 proof in alcoholic strength, that it is made mostly from rye malt and grain and "soft water from the rivers of the Moscow region," and has no additives such as sugar to alter its taste.

The problem is that, in common with all the vodkas exported by Sojuzplodoimport, the brand can be made by any of the 10 distilleries that are its shareholders even if they are

RATING
Moskovskaya Osobaya
★

Moskovskaya Cristall
★★

Moskovskaya Limon
★★

Flavoured Vodka
Imported from Russia

Moskovskaya

Limon

100% grain
neutral spirit and
natural lemon essence
produced and bottled in
the Cristall Distillery,
Moscow, Russia.

100 cl 40%vol (70° B.R. proof)

Exclusive Agent/Importer:
Plodimex GmbH D-Hamburg

outside the Moscow region. They have to follow a strict production process, but I very much doubt that they all use the same water.

The brand's production process is very similar to that of Stolichnaya. The rye malt and grain give it a slight sweetness and the water used is demineralized to make it smoother. It is also filtered three times through activated charcoal and quartz. The Limon version has natural essences of lemon added to the base spirit.

As is also the case with Stolichnaya, the brand has two line extensions, the deluxe Cristall and the lemon-flavored Limon, both of which are produced in the historic Cristall distillery in Moscow, which first came into operation in 1901 and is now Russia's largest.

ORIGINAL
RUSSIAN
VODKA

Moskovskaya
Cristall

*Moskovskaya Cristall is a
superlative vodka.
Pure and smooth and
crystal-clear.
From Russia's oldest-established
traditional vodka distillery.
An outstanding vodka for an
adventure in excellent taste.
Na zdorovie – Cheers!*

50 cl 40%vol (70° BR. proof)
Exclusive Agent/Importer:
Plodimex GmbH – D-2000 Hamburg 76

Distilled and bottled in Russia
for VVO Sojuzplodoimport, Moscow.

TASTING NOTES

MOSKOVSKAYA OSOBAYA

There are some impurities in the aroma, giving this vodka a slightly dank, unpleasant bouquet. Smooth on the palate to begin with and quite sweet, and then some aggressive alcohol burn begins to develop. Very short on the finish with very little lingering flavor and quite a lot of fire.

MOSKOVSKAYA CRISTALL

Very, very neutral on the nose with just hints of sweetness. Sweet, quite intense rye fragrance on the palate, slightly oily and with good initial smoothness. A bit short and slightly bitter on the finish. There is some alcohol burn and this gets stronger on the finish.

MOSKOVSKAYA LIMON

Honest, very pleasant, quite intense but subtle bouquet of lemons. Very smooth, pleasantly lemony, but not overpowering with a bit of needle. Nice, quite fragrant finish but a bit short.

Okhotnichya

SPIRIT FACTS

Owner V/O Sojuzplodoimport
Distillery several in Russia
Production figures not available
Strength 90 proof

Hunters in Eastern Europe have fortified themselves with vodka for centuries and Okhotnichya, or Hunter's Vodka, is a celebration of this tradition. Warm, spicy, and high in alcohol, it is just what you need after a cold day outdoors. The brand dates back only to the immediate post-war era, but the recipe is probably much older.

RATING

Okhotnichya
★★★★

The base spirit is infused with several unusual flavoring elements—ginger, tormentil, ashweed roots, clove, black and red peppers, juniper berries, coffee, aniseed, orange and lemon peel—and is then redistilled. It is then added to pure spirit and a little sugar and white port-style wine is blended in so that the wine makes up 20 percent of the final vodka.

TASTING NOTES

OKHOTNICHYA

Dark gold in color and very complex on the nose. The initial aroma is predominantly one of aniseed, but others, such as those of ginger and pepper, begin to be released as you swirl it around in the glass. Very smooth on the palate, a little oily, with a pleasant balance of dry and sweet flavors. A touch of fire from the extra alcohol to make it warming. Good persistence of flavor. Unlike any other vodka you will ever taste and, in my opinion, one of the best-flavored vodkas in the world.

Pertsovka

SPIRIT FACTS

Owner V/O Sojuzplodoimport
Distillery several in Russia
Production figures not available
Strengths 70, 80 proof

The flavoring of vodka with pepper is a tradition that goes back for centuries in both Russia and Poland, and that great vodka drinker, Peter the Great (1672–1725) always sprinkled some over his. The spice is said to be a great coagulant which also helps precipitate impurities to the bottom of the glass.

RATING

Pertsovka
★★

Today the Pertsovka brand is very popular in Russia and not surprisingly is often drunk as an antidote to a cold.

The brand is made by infusing high-quality grain spirit made in the usual Russian way with black and red pepper pods and cubeb berries. So why there is an illustration of red chiles on the label is a mystery to me. The vodka is then bottled at 70 or 80 proof.

TASTING NOTES

PERTSOVKA

This has the most beautiful color of any vodka I have ever seen, very bright, deep, golden brown with red tinges. On the nose, there are touches of aniseed and vanilla, but the predominant aroma is of spicy pepper. Initially surprisingly sweet but then hot and quite fiery with the peppery spice clinging to your gums and tongue. Extremely persistent in flavor.
I have tried to chill it down but this does little to dampen the hot, peppery flavors. You either love it or hate it!

Sibirskaya

SPIRIT FACTS

Owner V/O Sojuzplodoimport
Distillery several in Russia
Production 3.2 million cases
Strengths 75, 84, 90 proof

ORIGINAL
Siberian vodka

This is the classic Siberian-style vodka, although, as the brand is owned by Sojuzplodoimport, it can in theory be produced in any of the 10 distilleries that are the company's shareholders. It is, however, always produced following strict procedures and it is a vodka that is much revered in Russia. In fact it is the country's fourth-largest-selling brand with sales of 3.2 million cases.

RATING
Sibirskaya
★★★★

Only strong, healthy grain can survive Siberia's extremes of climate and this gives the vodka its sweetish, fragrant quality. The rectified spirit is then diluted with water from the region's unpolluted rivers, which has been demineralized to make the final spirit smoother. The final touch is multiple filtration through charcoal made from wild silver birch trees grown in the immense Taiga region.

TASTING NOTES

SIBIRSKAYA

Delicate, very light aroma, just slightly sweet. Big and fragrant in taste, quite sweet and almost creamily smooth until the extra alcohol begins to make itself felt and gives the vodka some bite. Nice long finish with some fire, but with a pleasant, lingering sweetness. An excellent vodka to be drunk neat and slightly chilled to take the edge off the alcohol.

Smirnoff Black

SPIRIT FACTS

Owner The Pierre Smirnoff Company
Distillery The Cristall Distillery, Moscow
Production figures not available
Strength 80 proof

The launch of Smirnoff Black in the mid-1990s was described by its producer, International Distillers & Vintners, owner of the Pierre Smirnoff Company, as the return of one of the world's greatest spirits brands to its spiritual home. Smirnoff Black is distilled in Moscow, from where Vladimir Smirnov (the family wrote its name with a "v" before the Revolution) had fled in the early stages of the Bolshevik Revolution, and it is produced using the same methods of distillation that were used in Russia at the time.

It was a fantastic volte-face by the company. For years we had been told that the Smirnoff produced in the West was distilled and purified according to the unique Smirnoff recipe and much was made of its heritage. But here was a

The Smirnov Distillery at 2 Piatnitskaya Street in Moscow, the pride of the Smirnov Company, later turned into a garage at the time of the Russian Revolution.

very different vodka and one portrayed as being far closer in style to the one the Smirnovs had distilled in Imperial Russia.

Smirnoff Black is distilled in the famous Cristall distillery in Moscow under the company's close supervision. It is made purely of grain but, instead of being produced in the usual continuous distillation and rectification apparatus, it is distilled in small batches in the traditional copper pot stills. This gives the master distiller far closer control over the process. And it also enables him to eliminate impurities but at the same time retain some of the natural flavors of the grain. The spirit is then filtered through silver-birch charcoal for purity and diluted with demineralized water.

This is a very different vodka from both its Red and Blue Label stablemates, one with a very definite character and aroma. So is it more akin to what the Smirnovs produced in Moscow than to the more neutral and lighter vodkas that the company produces in the West? I strongly suspect so.

Drink it neat and well chilled.

RATING
Smirnoff Black
★★★

TASTING NOTES

SMIRNOFF BLACK

Very light but discernible aroma of grain, not as neutral as the more established Russian brands but clean with just some hints of acetone.
Very smooth and a little oily, lovely and mellow with plenty of grain flavor. Nice long, flavorful finish. A bit of needle does develop but this is by no means unpleasant.
This is a very good vodka, one that is very Russian in style but with some Western influence discernible.

Smirnoff vodka began its life in Russia in 1818. Seventy-six years after the Revolution, in 1993, the Smirnoff distillery re-opened in Moscow. To commemorate this event, Smirnoff launched Smirnoff Black, the ultimate Russian vodka.

Stolichnaya

SPIRIT FACTS

Owner V/O Sojuzplodoimport
Distillery several in Russia
Production 15.12 million cases
Strengths 80 proof for all versions

Although its volume of production and sales has fluctuated wildly in recent years, Stolichnaya, or "Stoli" as it is usually known in the drinks industry, is still the largest vodka brand in the world with sales in 1995 estimated at just over 15.1 million cases. Most of this is consumed within Russia itself but the brand is now widely available all over the world.

The name means capital city in Russian and the illustration on the rather bleak label is of the Moscova Hotel, one of Moscow's most famous

Advertisement for Stolichnaya, the largest selling vodka brand in the world.

landmarks. As is the case with most Russian vodkas produced for export, however, the brand is made in all of the 10 distilleries that own the Sojuzplodoimport trading group. Only the deluxe Cristall and the lemon-flavored Limon lines are produced in a single plant—the famous Cristall (sometimes also spelled Kristall) distillery in Moscow which first started vodka production in 1901 and is now the largest in Russia.

RATING
Stolichnaya
★★
Stolichnaya Cristall
★★★
Stolichnaya Limon
★

Much of the Stolichnaya consumed in Russia is made from potatoes but the export version is made of grain, mostly wheat with a little bit of rye thrown in. The water used is what the Russians call "living" water, coming from natural sources such as rivers and lakes. It is treated to remove all the mineral content but is never distilled, so as not to spoil its naturally bright quality. A little sugar is then added to the spirit to make it smoother and it is filtered three times

Advertisement for Stolichnaya limon, produced in the famous Cristall distillery in Moscow.

through quartz and activated silver-birch charcoal. For the flavored version natural essences of lemon are added to the base spirit.

Stolichnaya was first produced as a brand in the 1950s and exports began about a decade later. The deluxe Cristall line was introduced in the early 1990s.

TASTING NOTES

STOLICHNAYA

So neutral that there is hardly any bouquet at all, but dig deep enough and some pleasant cereal aromas do come through. On the palate the sugar is evident, making this a rich vodka, but it does not quite disguise a slightly bitter background flavor. Nice and smooth, although some alcohol burn does develop when the spirit is rolled around on the tongue. Good rich finish but the needle is more persistent than the flavor.

STOLICHNAYA CRISTALL

More pungent than the mainstream brand with a greater concentration of alcohol and cereal aromas. Thicker and oilier in texture, quite smooth and mellow, although, again, some alcohol burn does develop. Sweetish with some caramelization. Light on the finish.

This is a very nice vodka, which is delicate and has less fire than the mainstream version.

STOLICHNAYA LIMON

Light in bouquet with very little aroma of lemon. Not very pleasant on the palate, with the light lemon flavor unable to disguise a slight sourness of taste. Bitterish finish with alcohol burn.

Ultraa

SPIRIT FACTS

Owner joint venture between Dethleffsen
and the Livis distillery
Distillery St Petersburg, Russia
Production figures not available
Strengths 75, 80 proof

The producers of this vodka describe it as a "modern world" Russian vodka and it is certainly lighter and cleaner than many other Russian brands. It is also refreshingly packaged in a modernistic bottle which has none of the pseudo-Czarist or -Stalinist imagery that is still so popular among Western producers.

Launched in 1995, Ultraa is the product of another East–West joint venture, this time between Dethleffsen, the German spirits producer, which produces the Rasputin vodka range, and the Livis distillery of St Petersburg. Livis is Russia's second-largest distillery producing more than 100 million bottles of vodka a year under different labels, and it is also one of the country's most advanced technologically.

Traditionally packaged it may not be, but the producers do claim to respect tradition. The recipe for the spirit is a traditional one and is said to date from the time of the Czars when Livis was a supplier to the Imperial Court. This is a vodka made purely of grain and the water used is drawn from Lake Ladoga to the north of St Petersburg, which has always had a reputation for purity. It is

RATING

Ultraa Vodka

★★

also renowned for its naturally high oxygen content, making it ideal for the production of clear and very bright vodkas. For good measure it is then filtered through quartz sand and semiprecious stones for extra purity. Once diluted to the right strength, the vodka is filtered through four activated charcoal filter columns.

The company claims that the Ontario Liquor Control Board, the largest single buyer in the world, gave it their highest rating. I would not rate it as highly, but this is a very good vodka, a halfway house between the old Russian traditional vodkas and those more akin to modern tastes.

The Livis distillery is open to visitors by prior arrangement.

TASTING NOTES

ULTRAA VODKA

The 80 proof version is lightish in aroma, very delicate and pleasant with a definite sweetness. Very slightly oily in texture, very smooth with only touches of needle. Sweet but just short of being cloying. Good persistence in the mouth.

This is a well-made vodka and I rate it highly on the quality level, although the style is a bit sweet for me. Serve it well chilled and neat. It is also light and clean enough to make a good, if not very dry, vodka Martini. Also suitable to go with mixers.

VODKA COCKTAILS

Although enjoyable on its own, vodka makes the perfect mixer for cocktails.
Here is merely a selection.

VODKA MARTINI

- ♦ Clear, preferably Western vodka
- ♦ Dry vermouth
- ♦ Olive, well rinsed, or zest of lemon

This is a variant to the classic Dry Martini made with gin and was made famous by James Bond with his "A vodka Martini. Very dry. Shaken, not stirred." Carefully made, the vodka version is a wonderful cocktail and, like the original, the epitome of sophistication, although, in my experience, I have never been able to re-create the dryness of the original. You can make it as dry as you like by varying the amount of vermouth added.

The slight sweetness of Eastern vodkas tends to clash with the flavor of the vermouth, so use a good, very dry Western brand. Tanqueray Sterling is my favorite, or one of the Nordics such as Finlandia or Absolut. Unless you want to be under the table after two use one with a strength of 80 proof. Go for 100 proof only if real dryness is what you are after but do not forget that high-proof vodkas, or any other spirit for that matter, have a "needle," a prickly sensation in the mouth.

Buy yourself a large freezer. Otherwise one that can fit several glasses, a shaker, and two bottles. Use the classic triangular cocktail glass if possible, otherwise one with a long stem so that the warmth of your hand does not reach the liquid.

Do not use ice, since this will dilute the spirit. Put the glass in the freezer for at least 10 minutes. It should frost over when you take it out. Chill the vodka until it is just below freezing and do the same with the dry vermouth. Most cognoscenti use the French Noilly Prat because its barrel aging gives it an extra dimension. But any good-quality, dry brand will do. How much vermouth you add to the vodka depends on how dry you want it to be. If you want it really, really dry, just, with a careful, steady hand, add a small dash; one-quarter of vermouth to three-quarters of vodka is probably how most people like it. Half and half is probably too sweet for most.

Bond fans will put the mixture into a cocktail shaker and this has the advantage of injecting a bit of fun into the process and aerating the spirit and bringing out the aromas. If you do use one, don't forget to chill it in the freezer as well.

Add a pitted green olive for decoration—it should fall to the bottom angle of the cocktail glass. Make sure that you rinse it thoroughly first, because most olives are packed in brine. Alternatively, add a thin curl of lemon zest about two inches long.

The **Et tu Brute** is a variant to this cocktail and is made by adding crème de cassis in equal measure to the vermouth. The **Churchill** is 15 parts of vodka to one of vermouth.

BITTER BISON

- ◆ Zubrowka Bison Grass vodka
- ◆ Sweet vermouth
- ◆ Lemon juice
- ◆ Ice

For those who like the classic, bison-grass-flavored Zubrowka from Poland, this is an interesting alternative to drinking it straight.

Put two or three lumps of ice into a tumbler. Pour over three measures of Zubrowka to one of sweet vermouth. Add a dash of lemon juice and decorate the glass with a lemon slice.

BLACK RUSSIAN

- ◆ Clear vodka
- ◆ Coffee liqueur
- ◆ Ice

Because of its name most will be tempted to use Russian vodka. Do so, but don't forget that the taste of the coffee liqueur will dominate and mask some of the vodka's subtleties of flavor.

Use a tumbler and put in two or three lumps of ice. Pour in two measure of vodka to one of coffee liqueur. Use a good liqueur, a Tia Maria or Kahlua.

A variant of this classic is the **Red Russian**, made with cranberry, preferably Finlandia, vodka rather than the clear one.

BLOODY MARY

- ◆ Clear vodka
- ◆ Tomato juice
- ◆ Worcestershire sauce
- ◆ Lemon juice
- ◆ Tabasco sauce
- ◆ Celery salt, stick of celery
- ◆ Ice

The classic hangover cure. When well prepared, however, this can be a wonderful morning cocktail, which is well worth keeping all the ingredients for.

Either a tumbler or a high glass can be used. Add a little ice, not too much. Pour in a large measure of vodka and top up with tomato juice. Add generous dashes of Worcester and Tabasco sauce and a little lemon juice. Then the celery salt or a long, narrow stick of fresh celery. Stir well. Alternatively use a shaker, strain, and put the celery stick in at the end.

BULL SHOT

- ♦ Clear vodka
- ♦ Consommé or beef bouillon
- ♦ Worcestershire sauce
- ♦ Lemon juice
- ♦ Celery salt
- ♦ Cayenne pepper
- ♦ Tabasco sauce

Don't bother to make this if all you have is a stock cube. The quality of this classic cocktail depends almost entirely on the quality of the consommé or bouillon so make sure that you get the best you can. It will pay off.

Put one measure of vodka and two of bouillon in a shaker. Add a dash of the sauces and lemon juice followed by the salt and pepper. Shake well and strain carefully into a tumbler or high glass.

CAIPIROSCA

- ♦ Clear, preferably Western vodka
- ♦ One lime, quartered
- ♦ White sugar
- ♦ Ice

Another variant of a national classic, this time the wonderfully refreshing *caipirinha* from Brazil, where it is made with the local *cachaca* cane spirit. Using vodka is a modern, trendy alternative.

Use a tumbler with a wide, heavy base that has been chilled in the freezer. Put a heaped tablespoon of sugar in the bottom of the glass, more if you want it sweeter. Add the limes and crush them with a pestle to get the juice out and loosen the pulp. Add two or three crushed ice cubes and top up with vodka. Mix well.

HARVEY WALLBANGER

♦ Clear vodka
♦ Orange juice
♦ Galliano
♦ Ice

The mixture of orange juice and vodka is probably best known in the **Screwdriver**, a simple, refreshing mixture of chilled orange juice and vodka served with ice in a tall glass. The Wallbanger is an interesting, more sophisticated version. Mix one measure of vodka with two of fresh orange juice and put in a tall glass with plenty of ice. Float two teaspoons of Galliano on the top and serve with straws.

LEAPER

♦ Clear vodka
♦ Cointreau
♦ Orange juice
♦ Maraschino cordial
♦ Black grape

This cocktail is not well known, but don't let that stop you. It looks and tastes wonderful. Make sure that you use chilled ingredients.

Mix one measure of vodka with two of Cointreau and add to the juice of two oranges. Put in a couple of dashes of the maraschino cordial and then shake well in a shaker before straining and pouring it into a classic cocktail glass. Put a cocktail stick or a toothpick through the grape and suspend it on top of the glass.

MOSCOW MULE

- ♦ Clear vodka
- ♦ Ginger beer
- ♦ Lemon juice or lime-juice cordial
- ♦ Sprig of mint
- ♦ Ice

More than any other, this was the cocktail that put vodka on the map in the United States and, although many dismiss it as a waste of vodka, it is still a classic. Use a Western vodka, preferably a Smirnoff, as that was the brand that was first used. Originally it was served in a copper mug, but now it is more often served in a tall glass.

Put in plenty of ice and a large measure of vodka. Top up with the ginger beer and add a generous slurp of lemon juice or lime-juice cordial. Decorate with a sprig of mint and drink through straws.

ROSE DE VARSOVIE

- ◆ Clear, Polish vodka
- ◆ Cherry cordial or Wisniowka cherry vodka
- ◆ Cointreau
- ◆ Angostura Bitters
- ◆ Cocktail cherry

Another for fans of Polish vodka. Very colorful but many will find it too sweet. Use the classic triangular cocktail glass and give the vodka, cherry cordial, and Cointreau a slight chill, but do not overdo it.

Then swirl the Angostura Bitters around in the glass and pour off any excess. Add three measures of vodka, definitely Polish vodka, with two of cherry cordial or Wisniowka and one of Cointreau. Allow the cocktail cherry to float down to the bottom angle of the glass.

SEA BREEZE

- ◆ Clear vodka
- ◆ Grapefruit juice
- ◆ Cranberry Juice

This is one of the most popular cocktails today. To two fingers of vodka, add two of cranberry juice and four of grapefruit juice. Serve in a tall, straight glass with ice and a squeeze of lime. Perfect refreshment for a summer's day.

VODKA WITH FOOD

Crayfish with rye bread and dill accompanies vodka in Scandinavia.

Vodka with food? To most Westerners this is a bizarre concept, one to be reserved for alcoholics only. But in the Nordic countries, in Poland and the countries of the old U.S.S.R. where vodka is the national spirit, they have been drinking vodka with food for centuries.

Cynics will argue that this is because wine, which many believe is good food's ideal companion, was expensive in these countries, while vodka was cheap and more accessible to most of the population. The truth, however, is more complicated and colorful than that. It has to be remembered that vodka's historic heartland—Poland, the countries of the old Russian empire, and Finland—was for most of its early history comparatively isolated from the rest of Europe and its wine culture. These countries developed their own national cuisine at the same time as their vodka industries were laying down roots. So it is not surprising that there should be a link between the two. The traditional Russian *zakuski* or snacks, for example, were first developed during the eighteenth century, when vodka production in the homes of the nobility reached a peak of excellence. The Russian aristocracy could well have afforded wine. But instead they drank vodka, often aromatized vodka, because they found that it suited the flavors and consistency of the food much better.

Today vodka is served with fish dishes across the region. But it is also drunk with a wide range of other dishes, particularly in Russia and Poland where the tradition of drinking vodka throughout a meal is still strong. Vodka does not go with everything. But to drink it with some of the hearty and spicy dishes of Eastern Europe is quite an experience.

CRAYFISH

In Finland and Sweden they have a very particular tradition. The crayfish season falls in high summer when the weather is warm and outdoor parties thrive during the long, warm nights. The crayfish are usually simply boiled, sometimes with the addition of dill, and served with plenty of rye bread and, in the case of Sweden, cheese. Ice-chilled vodka, with beer or mineral-water chasers, is the traditional accompaniment. It is an odd combination but the dry austerity of the spirit goes remarkably well with the sweet flesh of the shellfish.

CAVIARE AND FISH ROE

It is usually with saltier fish and fish products that vodka is recommended, however. The Russians have been enjoying vodka with caviare for generations and the combination is as evocative of the country as sable fur, *metrushka* dolls, and the Bolshoi Ballet. For, although caviare is regarded as one of the ultimate luxuries in the West, in Russia it remained comparatively cheap, even during the long night of Communism.

Russians enjoy caviare and fish roe with their vodka.

The vodka should be very cold and the caviare served with hot toast or *bliny*, a type of round pancake usually made from buckwheat that is common throughout Eastern Europe. Finely chopped raw onion and grated hard-cooked egg, sometimes with the yolk and white served separately, are sometimes also eaten as an accompaniment. Here it is the saltiness of the fish and the dryness of the vodka that enhance each other.

Caviare is a Russian product. In the Nordic countries and others of Eastern Europe it is usually other types of fish roe that are used, such as trout or salmon roe. Again this is often spread on *bliny* with sour cream, known as *smetana* in Finland, and chopped raw onion.

SMOKED AND SALTED FISH

Salmon and trout, either smoked or salted, are also eaten with vodka across the region. In Russia there is sturgeon and even pike and whitefish. But the most popular are herrings, usually from the Baltic.

Smoked and salted fish are also popular with vodka in Russia.

Again, these can be smoked or salted, but in Poland the traditional way is to marinate them in vinegar and then mix them with oil. Chopped onion and sour cream are frequent accompaniments, as are a range of sauces such as mustard or garlic.

Prepared in this way these fish dishes are usually hors d'oeuvres. When they are part of the main course they are usually served with plain boiled potatoes.

Zakuski in Russia and Zakaski in Poland—traditional vodka food.

ZAKUSKI OR ZAKASKI

On special occasions in Russia and Poland they drink vodka with most of their national dishes, even when these are made of meat: with roast suckling pig and kasha or buckwheat stuffing, with pelmeny or spiced meat dumplings, and with solianki, the thick, hot, spiced soups in Russia; with veal and cabbage dumplings served with sour cream or bigos, a type of sauerkraut, with meat, poultry, or sausages in Poland (the bison-grass-flavored Zubrowka brand goes particularly well); even with the national dish of duck with cranberries. The logic is immediately apparent. These are rich, heavy, full-flavored dishes that would swamp delicate beverages such as wine. But clear, chilled vodka more than holds its own against the strong flavors and helps to cut through the fattiness of the meat.

Salty tasting meats in aspic go well with vodka.

The great tradition, however, is to drink vodka with *zakuski* as they are known in Russia, or *zakaski* in Poland. "The main use of vodka in Russian cuisine is as an obligatory accompaniment to *zakuski*," claims William Pokhlebkin in his *History of Vodka*.

These are hot or cold snacks which the Russians and Poles lay out on a big table during a party or get-together and their range is enormous,

The dry taste of vodka goes well with the sweet flesh of shellfish.

rather like Spanish *tapas*. Served in small portions, all the fish or roe dishes mentioned are included in the range, but so too are meats and vegetables. There are too many to list here. The favorites, however, are mushrooms either plainly fried or tossed in breadcrumbs first; pickled cabbage or sauerkraut; and smoked meats such as ham and spicy sausages. And, in Russia, the slightly salty flavor of all sorts of meat in aspic goes particularly well with clear, chilled vodka. With the meats, radishes and mustard are also served to enhance the different flavors not only of the food but of the vodka as well.

Does this all sound a bit exotic for the Western palate? Then go into your local Russian or Polish restaurant and just do what the locals do— and what their ancestors did for generations before them.

TALL STORIES—VODKA ANECDOTES

Vodka is a drink with a rich history, so it is not surprising that many anecdotes have grown up around it. Here is just a selection.

———◆———

The Russian academic William Pokhlebkin has gone to great lengths to prove that vodka is a Russian invention (see p.25). He even has a stab at identifying its first distiller.

The Thessalian Greek cleric Isidor was a member of the Russian church legation that visited Italy at the end of the 1430s and visited a number of Italian monasteries where they could have seen aqua vitae *being distilled.*

On their return Isidor was imprisoned in the monastery of Chudov, having incurred the wrath of Vasily III. Curiously, he was not burned and, even more curiously, he was imprisoned under good conditions. One year later he escaped unhindered and was able to obtain transport to leave the Moscow state unpursued by Vasily. Pokhlebkin writes:

> *It is entirely possible that, wishing to save his life, Isidor, an extremely astute Greek, succeeded in carrying out alcohol distillation on an experimental basis in the Chudov monastery; and that, not having any other raw material, he settled on the use of grain. If Isidor did indeed prepare alcoholic spirit … this might have made it easier for him to lull the guards to sleep and escape the monastery.*

———◆———

The Moscow Mule cocktail did much to make vodka popular in the U.S.A. but, during the Korean War (1950–1953), its name and the fact that it was made from what was considered a Russian spirit came in for criticism from American patriots. The Bartenders Union even staged a parade on Fifth Avenue in New York carrying banners with the slogan, "We can do without the Moscow Mule." Heublein, the producer of Smirnoff, had to hastily issue a statement informing the country that, far from being produced in Russia, it was distilled in Connecticut in the heart of New England, the perennial stronghold of American patriotism. Screwdrivers are a well-known cocktail made by mixing vodka with orange juice. They are said to have been invented by American engineers in the Middle East, who mixed the drink with their screwdrivers.

When vodka was first distilled in Sweden, its main purpose was medicinal and it was drunk from a spoon. A fifteenth-century Swedish document claimed that it could cure more than forty ailments including headache, head lice, kidney stones, and toothache. It also suggested that it was "good for women that are infertile."

———◆———

In 1648 the "tavern revolts" in Moscow and other Russian cities brought to an end the system of "Czar's taverns," which gave the exclusive right to tavern keepers to produce and sell vodka. The riots are said to have been caused by the fall in quality of vodka as tavern keepers cut corners to save money; the growing debts that the urban poor owed to tavern keepers; and the calamitous effects of drunkenness in rural areas where the peasantry's overindulgence in vodka at Easter resulted in several years of crop failures.

———◆———

Peter I ("the Great") of Russia (1672–1725) was a great vodka drinker, his favorite being one flavored with anise. During his frequent visits abroad he always took a stock with him and, while on a visit to the palace of Versailles in France in 1717, he wrote to the Czarina complaining that he was down to his last bottle. He also ensured that others enjoyed it, granting a free cup of vodka a day to all road workers, soldiers, sailors, stevedores, and shipyard workers.

The same monarch, known as the "merry Czar" but one who used vodka ruthlessly as a political instrument, also invented the "penalty cup." Noblemen, military leaders, or important politicians who incurred his displeasure were summoned to appear before him and his court in all their finery and accompanied by their servants. They were then forced to drink a cup of vodka containing two pints before the jeering courtiers. The resulting public drunkenness was supposed to strip them of all their dignity and sometimes resulted in death.

———◆———

The quality of Russian vodka produced in aristocratic households during the reign of Catherine II ("the Great") (1729–1796) was so good that the Czarina gave gifts of it to foreign rulers, including Gustav III of Sweden and Frederick the Great of Prussia. She also sent some of it to the French philosopher Voltaire, who was well known to be fond of fine wines. When a courtier expressed his doubts on the wisdom of this she replied, "After this he will swallow his tongue whether from surprise or delight or out of envy for Russia."

The Smirnov family began distilling vodka in Moscow in 1818. Their big breakthrough, however, came in 1886 at the Nizhni Novgorod exhibition, Russia's largest trade fair, when Czar Alexander III appointed them purveyors to the imperial court. His attention is said to have been caught by Piotr Smirnov's ploy of having a real bear in his pavilion and by dressing up his waiters in bear costumes to serve the vodka.

———◆———

Brännvin Companies with the exclusivity to serve and sell vodka through special restaurants were formed throughout Sweden in the second half of the nineteenth century (see p.40). Their aim was to promote sobriety, good morals, and better living conditions for the working man, but this proved difficult to achieve.

The following is a description of a company restaurant published by the *Göteborgs-Posten* newspaper in 1897:

Saturday, December 11, 6 P.M. ... We enter the premises. The air is so nauseating and disgusting and I have the immediate urge to turn and run out again. But I force myself not to and we sit down at a table in the room on the clumsy yellow chairs without backs. One of us forces his way through the crowds of spirit-hungry men packed around the bar and orders coffee and brännvin, which we soon receive ... A thought flashes through my mind suddenly about the wonderful aspirations of the forefathers of the System of turning the restaurant into a good, clean neighbourhood eating place for the working class. But, in this place, an excellent appetite is surely needed ...

———◆———

There is a popular saying in Poland that "Vodka drunk in moderation is harmless ... even when drunk in the largest quantities."

———◆———

There are thousands of jokes about vodka in Poland and one of the most popular is the one about an alcoholic who decides to rid himself of his problem. When he tells his doctor that his consumption is about one pint per day, the doctor's advice is to reduce this to two or three glasses and to come back and see him in two weeks.

A fortnight later he returns and the doctor sees immediately that he is very drunk. "Did you take your doctor's advice and reduce your intake to two or three glasses?" he asks. "Yes," replies the man. "But you're not my only doctor."

Polaroid Instant Cameras, which produced photos within minutes of their being taken, played their part in vodka's growth in popularity in the U.S. During the 1950s John G. Martin, the famous president of Heublein Corporation, which launched Smirnoff in the country (see p.47), used to carry one around with him when doing the rounds of the bars. He used to take two photographs of the bartender making a Moscow Mule and give one of them to him. The other he took to his next port of call to persuade the next barman that everyone was drinking what was at the time a little-known cocktail.

The original Martini cocktail was made with gin, that most quint-essential of English spirits. So it is paradoxical that one of the most famous ambassadors of the vodka Martini in the 1950s and 1960s was that great British cold-war warrior James Bond. "A vodka Martini. Very dry. Shaken, not stirred." Just as paradoxical is that the actor who first played the part is a Scottish Nationalist who drinks whisky.

Bond did not only drink vodka Martinis. In *Casino Royale* he orders a cocktail made from three measures of Gordon's gin, one of vodka, and a half-measure of Kina Lilet, all of it shaken and ice-cold with a large slice of lemon. "Gosh, that's certainly a drink," comments his friend Felix Leiter. "I never have more than one drink before dinner," Bond replies. "But I do like that one to be large and very strong and very cold and very well made."

Glossary

activated charcoal/carbon Charcoal or carbon that has been heated up to make it more absorbent and more efficient in filtration.

analyzer The first column of a continuous still that extracts most of the alcohol from the wash.

bliny Pancakes from Eastern Europe often served as an accompaniment to vodka with sour cream or caviare and other fish products.

brännvin Literally "burned wine," a spirit originally produced in Sweden by the distillation of wine. By the seventeenth century it was used to denote a spirit produced from a cereal base.

burn A harsh, astringent and puckering sensation in the mouth caused by the alcohol. Often found in cheap vodkas or those with a high level of alcohol.

caramelization The burning of unfermented sugars from the wash in the still that gives vodka a sweet, cloying taste of caramel or toffee. A common fault in vodkas produced by fast, continuous distillation.

carbon A derivative of charcoal, in widespread use for filtration.

coagulants Materials, such as milk and egg whites, used in times past for the filtration of vodka. They coat the impurities of the spirit and bring them to the surface where they can then be skimmed off.

congeners Also known as congenerics. The elements that impart taste to a spirit.

continuous stills Also known as patent or Coffey stills. The most commonly used apparatus in vodka production today, they distill the wash then rectify it in a continuous process using a minimum of two columns.

crisp Lacking in any sweetness of flavor or any heaviness of texture.

ethyl alcohol The potable, clean variety of alcohol. Other varieties are less clean smelling, such as amyl alcohol that has an odor akin to that of nail varnish.

finish The aftertaste of a vodka or the sensation and taste left in the mouth after it has been swallowed.

fusel oil A thick, greasy element created in the fermentation process. As it is not harmful in small quantities, some distillers leave a little of it in their vodka to add smoothness.

ions Hard minerals often present in water that impart roughness to the final vodka.

"luxury" vodka A Polish vodka produced in a single Polmos that has worldwide rights to the brand.

mouth feel The weight and texture of a vodka in the mouth.

needle A slight prickle on the tongue caused by the alcohol in vodka. This is not necessarily a fault but it should never be harsh or rough.

nose (*vb*) The careful smelling of a vodka or any other spirit, usually with the help of a tasting glass.

Polmos A state-owned vodka production center in Poland. At time of writing there are 25 of these in the country which buy in raw alcohol from agricultural distilleries and rectify, filter and bottle it as vodka. These Polmoses jointly own the rights to most of the leading Polish vodka brands such as Wyborowa, and Jarzębiak.

rectifier The second column of a continuous still that extracts impurities from the alcohol produced in the analyzer.

stopki A long, thin glass with a stem, used for vodka drinking in Russia.

wash A beer-like liquid with an alcoholic strength of 12–16 proof, produced by the fermentation of a mixture of water, cereal or potatoes, and yeast. It is then converted into raw spirit by distillation.

zanuski A wide range of snacks, made from anything from meat to fish to vegetables, often used to accompany vodka drinking in Russia. Known as zakaski in Poland.

PICTURE CREDITS
p.9 The Pierre Smirnoff Company, p.17 Primalco International Brands, p.18 Vin & Spirit, p.19 Wine and Spirit Education Trust, p.28 ET Archive, p.37 Rajamäki Museum, p.41 Vin & Spirit Museum, p.42 Vin & Spirit Museum, p.46 The Pierre Smirnoff Company, p.47 The Pierre Smirnoff Company, pp.58–9 Life File, p.72 Alko Ltd/Exports, p.102 Alko Ltd/Exports, p.113 The Pierre Smirnoff Company, p.115 The Pierre Smirnoff Company, p.116 The Pierre Smirnoff Company, p.126 Alko Ltd/Exports, pp.128–9 Life File, p.134 Department of Portraits, The Royal College of Music, p.145 Alko Ltd/Exports, p.156 Life File, p.165 The Pierre Smirnoff Company.

ACKNOWLEDGMENTS
As well as all the vodka producers featured in this book that helped with information and samples, I would like to thank the following: Sally Green, my editor, for her patience; Adrian Donner, of Primalco, for his help on the section on Finland; Erik Juul-Mortensen, of Danisco Distillers, who put the case for Denmark; Dave Steward, of Marblehead Brand Development, for his humor and enthusiasm; Wanda Moscicka, of Agros, whose knowledge of the Polish vodka industry was invaluable; Jaroslaw Mazur, of the same company, who drove me to Poznan; Hugh Williams, master distiller at United Distillers, Laindon, who shed light on the mysteries of spirits production; Toby Fox, editor of *SpiritScan*, and Chris Losh, features editor of *Wine & Spirit International*, for their help with background information on the different brands; Alun Williams, for his help and opinions during innumerable and often unforgettable tasting sessions; and, last but not least, my wife France and daughter Arabella, for putting up with it all.

Index

Absolut 9, 43, 60-3
Agros Trading 129
akvavit 44
alcoholic strength 56
Alko 86
Altaï Siberian 158
Arcus Produkter 123
Aslanov 64-6

Barclay's 67
Barton 68-9
Barton Brands 47, 67, 68–9, 75,
    76, 89, 92, 101, 110, 112
Belgian vodkas 64-6, 99, 121
Belvédère 130
Berentzen 103-5
Bitter Bison (cocktail) 174
Black Death 70
Black Russian (cocktail) 174-5
Blavod 71-2
Bloody Mary 175
Boisset group 80, 98
Bols 131-2
Bruggeman, Distillers 64

Catco 84, 120
caviare 181-2
cherry flavoring 149
Chopin 133-4
cocktails 172-9
Coffey still 17-19
Cossack 73
Cracovia 135
crayfish 181
Cristall Distillery 165, 168
Cristalnaya 74
Crystal Palace 75
Czarina 76

Danisco Distillers 77-9, 91
Danish vodkas 44, 77-9, 91
Danzka 77-9
Dethleffsen 106-8, 170
distillation
    history of 14-15
    process 16-20

1822 80-3
Eldurís 84-5
Estonian vodka 100

Fiddler 136
filtration & purification 21-2
Finlandia 9, 39, 86-8
Finnish vodkas 37-9, 86-8
fish, smoked & salted 182-3
flavored vodkas 49-52
Fleishmann's 89
Fourcroy 99
French Alps 90
French vodkas 80-3, 90, 98
Frïs 53, 91

German vodkas 45, 93-4, 103-8
Glenmore 92
Gorbatschow 45, 93
Gordon's 47, 95-6
grain vodkas 11-12

Harvey Wallbanger 177
Henkell & Söhnlein 94
Heublin 8, 47
Heyman Distillers 71
Hooghoudt Distillers 45, 109
Hunter's Vodka (Okhotnichya) 31,
    51, 162
Huzzar 97

Icelandic vodkas 84-5, 120
Ikonova 98
impurities 56
Irish vodkas 97
Iskra 99

Jarzębiak 36, 51, 137

Koskenkorva 38, 39
Kraków, Polmos 35, 135, 136
Krepkaya 159
Królewska 138
Krupnik 139
Kunett, Rudolf 46-7, 115

INDEX

Leaper (cocktail) 177
Livis Distillery 170-1
Luksusowa 140

Martin, John G. 9, 47, 48
molasses vodka 12-13
Monopol 100
Morin company 80-2
Moscow Mule (cocktail) 47, 178
Moskovskaya 31
Moskovskaya Osobaya 160-1
Mr Boston 101-2

Netherlands vodkas 44-5, 109
Norwegian vodkas 123-4

Okhotnichya 31, 51, 162
Original Black Vodka Co 71

Pani Twardowska 141-2
Pernod Ricard Altaï 158
Pertsovka 31, 163
Pieprzówka 134
Polish vodkas 10, 128-55
  character of 24
  history of 32-7
Poznan, Polmos 35, 144-6, 151
potato vodka 12
Premium 144-6
proof system 56
Puschkin 103-5

Rajamäki 37-9
Rasputin 106-8
rectification 18-20
Remedia 100
Richmond Distillers 70, 74, 111
Rives Pitman 122
Rose de Varsovie (cocktail) 179
Royalty 45, 53, 109
Russian vodkas 10, 157-71
  character 24
  history of 25-31
rye vodka 11-12

Sea Breeze (cocktail) 179
serving vodka 53-4
Schenley 110
Selekt 111

Sibirskaya 31, 164
Siedlce, Polmos 133-4
Skol 112
Smirnoff 8, 113-16
Smirnoff Black 31, 165-6
Smirnoff family 46-7, 113-15
Smith, Lars Olsson 43,60
Sojuzplodoimport 157, 159, 160, 162, 163, 164, 167
Spanish vodka 122
Starka 147-8
Sterling 53, 117-19
Stolichnaya 31, 167-9
Swedish vodka 40-3, 60-3

Tanqueray Stirling 53,117-19
tasting 54,55
Tindavodka 120

U.K. vodkas 70-4, 111, 117-19, 125-6
Ultraa 170-1
Unicom-Bols Group 131-141
United Distillers 47, 73, 95, 118
U.S. vodkas 8-9, 23-4, 46-8, 67-9, 75-6, 89, 92, 95, 112

V & S 60
Van Hoo 121
Vikingfjord 123-4
Virgin 125-6
Vladivar 127
Vodka Martini 172-3
Von Haupold 122

water, in vodka production 13
Western style vodka 8-10, 23-4, 44-8, 58-127
Whyte & Mackay 127
Wiśniówka 35, 149
Wolfschmidt 45, 46, 48
Wyborowa 36, 150-2

zakuski 183-4
Zielona Góra, Polmos 35, 138, 151
Zubrowka 153-4
Zyrardów, Polmos 130
Zytnia, Extra 155